GOVERNMENT BULLIES

How Everyday Americans Are Being Harassed, Abused, and Imprisoned by the Feds

★ ★ ★ ★

SENATOR RAND PAUL

with Doug Stafford

CENTER
STREET

New York • Boston • Nashville

Center Street
Hachette Book Group
237 Park Avenue
New York, NY 10017

www.CenterStreet.com

Printed in the United States of America

RRD-C

First edition: September 2012

10 9 8 7 6 5 4

Center Street is a division of Hachette Book Group, Inc.
The Center Street name and logo are trademarks of
Hachette Book Group, Inc.

The Hachette Speakers Bureau provides a wide range of authors for speaking events. To find out more, go to www.HachetteSpeakersBureau.com or call (866) 376-6591.

The publisher is not responsible for websites (or their content) that are not owned by the publisher.

Library of Congress Control Number: 2012942779
ISBN: 9781455522750

*I dedicate this book to my mother
and my father...*

*From the age of eleven, I followed my father everywhere.
I listened to every speech and interview, thousands of them.
Are individualists born or nurtured? I think I was both. But
for every avenue that my father and I share—medicine, politics,
biking, to name a few—there exists a quieter yet equally
powerful influence without which I would not be who I am and
this book could not have come forth. That force comes from my
mother. Mothers never get enough credit. So, Mom and Dad.
Here's to you—a million thanks.*

Contents

Foreword by Ron Paul

The sole purpose of government is to protect our liberties. But today we have a government that has too often become the enemy of liberty. The Constitution is supposed to restrain and limit the government's power. But every day our government behaves as if it has no limits on its power.

How our government regularly abuses American citizens and ignores their rights would've outraged our Founding Fathers. They did not fight a revolution against a tyrannical government in faraway England simply to implement the same kind of government on their own soil. As Benjamin Franklin famously said and our Founders knew well, those who trade liberty for security get neither.

Freedom is not defined by safety. Freedom is defined by the ability of citizens to live without government interference. Government cannot create a world without risks, nor would we really wish to live in such a fictional place. Only a totalitarian society would even claim absolute safety as a worthy ideal, because it would require total state control over its citizens' lives. Liberty has meaning only if we still believe in it when terrible things happen and a false government security blanket beckons.

Rand has compiled stories in this book that sound as if they took place under a tyrannical dictatorship, not in the world's self-proclaimed freest nation. Our government now throws people in jail just for trying to make improvements to their own property. It seizes materials from private businesses and issues draconian fines. It gropes and humiliates travelers as standard policy. Washington, D.C., even tells us what kind of milk we can and cannot drink.

What we can say, do, or think has somehow now become the government's business. It's as if the Constitution and the Bill of Rights never even existed.

The ways in which government abuses us is rampant. Rand will tell you the story of the Sackett family, who took on the Environmental Protection Agency in a case of blatant federal agency overreach and abuse of private property rights. Without any proof or reason, and no chance for appeal, the EPA determined that the Sacketts' small single-home lot was a "protected wetland." The Sacketts were ordered to halt construction already under way, to remove all of the work already done, and to plant trees and shrubs consistent with a wetlands environment. After making these costly changes, the Sacketts then would have to wait several years for the EPA to decide if they would be allowed to use their own property. Refusal to comply with these outrageous and arbitrary commandments would result in daily fines greater than the value of the property!

My own district in Texas is no stranger to these issues, and has suffered from similar government decrees not unlike those imposed through elastic definitions of "wetland." Again, with no evidence to support their decision, the EPA arbitrarily determined Matagorda County to be an "Ozone Nonattainment Region," meaning its air quality is substandard. In fact, the population in the county has been decreasing and the small quantity of emissions reported from it has actually declined in recent years. The Texas agency charged with environmental protection disagrees with the EPA. Yet Matagorda County, like the Sacketts, finds itself at the mercy of the EPA. New business and construction will be stymied until the Washington masters are satisfied.

Unless Congress does something about this, EPA bureaucrats will continue to inflict potentially devastating economic consequences on communities like Matagorda County and people like the Sacketts. Destroying the economy is no way to save the environment. A thriving economy and a fair judicial system that respects property rights and the Constitution provide the best protection for the environment.

Unfortunately, our government currently has about as much use for justice or fairness as it does for the Constitution itself. Just take a look at what it currently thinks about the Fourth Amendment. The Fourth Amendment states, "The right of the people to be secure in their persons, houses, papers, and effects, against unreasonable searches and seizures, shall not be violated, and no Warrants shall issue, but upon probable cause, supported by Oath or affirmation, and particularly describing the place to be searched, and the persons or things to be seized."

We are not "secure" in any reasonable sense if an agency like the EPA can target innocent citizens and ruin their lives. We are certainly no longer protected from "unreasonable searches," an act the Transportation Security Administration now considers standard practice. Rand was stopped and harassed last year by the TSA, something he recounts in this book. Much worse are the horror stories he tells of Americans being abused in a much harsher manner, all in the name of "safety."

The growing revolt against invasive TSA practices is encouraging to Americans who are fed up with federal government encroachment in their lives. In the case of air travelers, this encroachment is quite literally physical. Fortunately, a deepseated libertarian impulse still exists within the American people, and opposition to the implementation of the TSA full-body scanners and groping searches proves that such sentiment is gathering momentum.

Rand and I both have introduced legislation to get rid of the TSA and limit its ability to harass citizens. I introduced legislation based on a very simple principle: Federal agents should be subject to the same laws as ordinary citizens. If you would face criminal prosecution or a lawsuit for groping someone, exposing them to unwelcome radiation, causing them emotional distress, or violating indecency laws, then TSA agents should similarly face sanctions for their actions.

This principle goes beyond TSA agents, however. As commentator Lew Rockwell has noted, the bill "enshrines the key lesson of the freedom philosophy: the government is not above the moral law. If it is wrong for you and me, it is wrong for people in government suits.... That is true of TSA crimes too." The revolt against TSA also serves as a refreshing reminder that we should not give in to government alarmism or be afraid to question government policies.

Certainly, those who choose to refuse the humiliating and potentially harmful full-body scanner machines may suffer delays, inconveniences, or worse. But I still believe peaceful resistance is the most effective tool against federal encroachment on our constitutional rights, which leads me to be supportive of any kind of "opt-out" or similar popular movements.

After all, what price can we place on our dignity, personal

privacy, and physical integrity? We have a right not to be treated like criminals and searched by federal agents without some reasonable evidence of criminal activity. Are we now to accept that merely wishing to travel and board an aircraft give rise to reasonable suspicion of criminality?

Also, let's not forget that the TSA was created in the aftermath of 9/11, when far too many Americans were clamoring for government protection from the specter of terrorism. Indeed it was congressional Republicans, the majority party in 2001, who must bear much of the blame for creating the Department of Homeland Security and TSA in the first place. Congressional Republicans also overwhelmingly supported the Patriot Act, which added to the atmosphere of hostility toward civil liberties in the name of state-provided "security."

But as we've seen with the TSA, federal "security" has more to do with humiliation and control than making us safe. It has more to do with instilling a mindset of subservience, which is why laughable policies such as removing one's shoes continue to be enforced. What else could explain the shabby, degrading spectacle of a line of normally upbeat Americans shuffling obediently through airport security in their stocking feet?

Computer security specialist Bruce Schneier has called much of what government agencies like the TSA do "security theater," which means all the harassment and abuse of innocent citizens is intended to give the illusion of safer travel while nothing is really being done to make this a reality.

And consider what the TSA actually does on a regular basis. The press reports are horrifying: ninety-five-year-old women humiliated; children molested; disabled people abused; men and women subjected to unwarranted groping and touching of their most private areas; involuntary radiation exposure. If the perpetrators were a gang of criminals, their headquarters would be raided by SWAT teams and armed federal agents. Unfortunately, in this case the perpetrators *are* armed federal agents.

The requirement that Americans be forced to undergo this appalling treatment simply for the "privilege" of traveling in their own country reveals much about how the federal government feels about our liberties. The unfortunate fact that we put up with this does not speak well for our willingness to stand up to an abusive government.

Many Americans continue to fool themselves into accepting TSA abuse by saying, "I don't mind giving up my freedoms for security." In fact, they are giving up their liberties and not receiving security in return. Consider some of the stories we've heard: An elderly cancer victim was forced to submit to a cruel and pointless TSA search, including removal of an adult diaper, yet a Nigerian immigrant somehow managed to stroll through TSA security checks and board a flight from New York to Los Angeles—with a stolen, expired boarding pass and an out-of-date student ID as his sole identification! He was detained and questioned, only to be released to do it again five days later! We should not be surprised to find government ineptitude and indifference at the TSA.

At the time the TSA was being created I strongly opposed federalization of airline security. As I wrote in an article back in 2001:

> Congress should be privatizing rather than nationalizing airport security. The free market can and does produce excellent security in many industries. Many security-intensive industries do an outstanding job of

maintaining safety without depending on federal agencies. Nuclear power plants, chemical plants, oil refineries, and armored money transport companies all employ private security forces that operate very effectively. No government agency will ever care about the bottom-line security and profitability of the airlines more than the airlines themselves. Airlines cannot make money if travelers and flight crews are afraid to fly, and in a free market they would drastically change security measures to prevent future tragedies. In the current regulatory environment, however, the airlines prefer to relinquish all responsibility for security to the government, so that they cannot be held accountable for lapses in the future.

What we need is real privatization of security, but not phony privatization with the same TSA screeners in private security firm uniforms still operating under the "guidance" of the federal government. Real security will be achieved when the airlines are once again in charge of protecting their property and their passengers.

If the TSA is busy fooling us into believing it is keeping us safe from terrorists, other government agencies also try to make us believe they are protecting us from ourselves. The Food and Drug Administration and U.S. Department of Agriculture are perfect examples of supposedly well-intentioned government run amok.

In this book, Rand tells the story of Dan Allgyer. After a yearlong undercover sting operation, armed federal agents acting on behalf of the FDA raided the business of this Pennsylvanian Amish farmer to prevent him from selling his unpasteurized milk to willing, fully informed customers in

Maryland. Federal agents wasted a whole year and who knows how many of our tax dollars posing as customers in order to catch Allgyer committing the "crime" of selling his milk. He was not tricking people into buying it, he was not forcing people to purchase it, and there had been no complaints about his product. These were completely voluntary transactions, but ones that our nanny-state federal government did not approve of, and so they shut down his business. The arrogance of the FDA and so many other federal agencies is simply appalling. These types of police-state raids on peaceful businessmen have no place in a free society.

The FDA claims its regulatory powers over food safety give it the authority to ban the interstate sales of raw milk, but this is an unconstitutional misapplication of the commerce clause.

The drafters of the Constitution separated powers between the legislative executive, and judiciary branches as a means of protecting the people from concentrations of power. Today the separation of powers, for all practical purposes, no longer exists. If the executive branch feels hamstrung by the fact that our framers placed lawmaking authority in the legislative branch, they simply make their own laws and call them "regulations." We all know how the EPA uses such bogus regulation authority to harass, hinder, and shut down countless other legitimate businesses. Sadly, Congress has been far too lax for far too long as the executive branch continues to encroach on its areas of responsibility and thereby undermine our system of government.

Most Americans understand that if you don't want to drink unpasteurized milk you simply do not buy it. But the federal government solution is predawn raids that destroy the livelihoods of honest, hardworking families.

I was outraged by this raid and the many others like it, and introduced a bill to allow the shipment and distribution of unpasteurized milk and milk products for human consumption across state lines. This legislation would remove the unconstitutional restraint on farmers who wish to sell or otherwise distribute, and people who wish to consume, unpasteurized milk and milk products.

Americans have the right to consume these products without having the federal government second-guess their judgment or thwart their wishes. If there are legitimate concerns about the safety of unpasteurized milk, those should be addressed at the state and local level. Many Americans have done their own research and come to the conclusion that unpasteurized milk is healthier than pasteurized.

Citizens doing their own research on what they put into their bodies, learning about what they eat, drink, or take for medicinal purposes—this information is often blocked by agencies like the FDA, a clear violation of the First Amendment.

In 2011, I gave the following speech on the House floor:

Mr. Speaker, I rise to introduce two pieces of legislation restoring the First Amendment rights of consumers to receive truthful information regarding the benefits of foods and dietary supplements. The first bill, the Health Freedom Restoration Act, codifies the First Amendment by ending the Food and Drug Administration's efforts to censor truthful health claims. The second bill, the Freedom of Health Speech Act, codifies the First and Fifth Amendments by requiring the Federal Trade Commission to prove that health claims are false before it takes action to stop manufactures and marketers from making the claims.

The American people have made it clear they do not want the federal government to interfere with their access to dietary supplements, yet the FDA and the FTC continue to engage in heavy-handed attempts to restrict such access. The FDA continues to frustrate consumers' efforts to learn how they can improve their health even after Congress, responding to a record number of constituents' comments, passed the Dietary Supplement and Health and Education Act of 1994 (DSHEA). FDA bureaucrats are so determined to frustrate consumers' access to truthful information that they are even evading their duty to comply with four federal court decisions vindicating consumers' First Amendment rights to discover the health benefits of foods and dietary supplements.

FDA bureaucrats have even refused to abide by the DSHEA section allowing the public to have access to scientific articles and publications regarding the role of nutrients in treating diseases by claiming that every article concerning this topic is evidence of intent to sell an unapproved and unlawful drug.

Because of the FDA's censorship of truthful health claims, millions of Americans may suffer with diseases and other health care problems they may have avoided by using dietary supplements. For example, the FDA prohibited consumers from learning how folic acid reduces the risk of neural tube defects for four years after the Centers for Disease Control and Prevention recommended every woman of childbearing age take folic acid supplements to reduce neural tube defects. This FDA action contributed to an estimated 10,000 cases of preventable neural tube defects!

The FDA also continues to prohibit consumers from learning about the scientific evidence that glucosamine and chondroitin sulfate are effective in the treatment of osteoarthritis; that omega-3 fatty acids may reduce the risk of sudden death heart attack; that calcium may reduce the risk of bone fractures; and that vitamin D may reduce the risk of osteoporosis, hypertension, and cancer.

The Health Freedom Restoration Act will force the FDA to at last comply with the commands of Congress, the First Amendment, numerous federal courts, and the American people by codifying the First Amendment prohibition on prior restraint. Specifically, the Health Freedom Restoration Act stops the FDA from censoring truthful claims about the curative, mitigative, or preventative effects of dietary supplements. The Health Freedom Restoration Act also stops the FDA from prohibiting the distribution of scientific articles and publications regarding the role of nutrients in protecting against disease. The FDA has proven that it cannot be trusted to protect consumers' rights to make informed choices. It is time for Congress to stop the FDA from censoring truthful health information.

The Freedom of Health Speech Act addresses the FTC's violations of the First Amendment. Under traditional constitutional standards, the federal government bears the burden of proving an advertising statement false before censoring that statement. However, the FTC shifted the burden of proof to industry. The FTC presumes health advertising is false and compels private parties to prove the ads (and everything the regulators say the ads imply) to be true to a near-conclusive degree. This violation of the First and Fifth Amendments is harming consumers by blocking innovation in the health foods and dietary supplement marketplace.

The Freedom of Health Speech Act requires the government to actually prove that speech is false before the FTC acts against the speaker. This is how it should be in a free society where information flows freely in order to foster the continuous improvement that benefits us all. The bill also requires that the FTC warn parties that their advertising is false and give them a chance to correct their mistakes before the FTC censors the claim and imposes other punishments.

Mr. Speaker, if we are serious about putting people in charge of their health care, then shouldn't we stop federal bureaucrats from preventing Americans from learning about simple ways to improve their health? I therefore call on my colleagues to stand up for good health and the Constitution by cosponsoring the Health Freedom Restoration Act and the Freedom of Health Speech Act.

The same year I also introduced the Testimonial Free Speech Act, legislation that would prohibit the federal government from censoring an individual's account of his experience with foods and dietary supplements. Hard as it may be to believe, the government is prohibiting individuals from sharing their stories of how they improved their health by using foods and dietary supplements.

In 2011, armed federal agents raided the headquarters of

Maxam Nutraceutics, a company that produces and sells nutritional supplements for people with autism spectrum disorder and Alzheimer's disease. The raid was based on Maxam's alleged failure (a failure Maxam CEO James Cole disputes) to comply with a warning letter from the FDA ordering Maxam to remove several "improper labels" from Maxam products. The labels in question were simply accounts from Maxam customers describing their experiences with Maxam products.

That's right—the federal government sent armed agents into a private business because the business posted customers' testimonials.

Restricting communication of individuals' accounts of their experiences with foods and dietary supplements is a blatant violation of the First Amendment. The necessity for my bill showed how little respect the federal bureaucracy has for the Bill of Rights and the principles of a free society. If we are not even free anymore to decide something as basic as what we wish to eat or drink or what medicine to take—or allowed to discuss it with our fellow Americans—how much freedom do we really have left?

During my presidential campaigns in 2008 and 2012, I could tell people were fed up. Americans are tired of a government that thinks it can dictate every detail of their daily lives. Citizens are tired of government getting in the way of hardworking people's efforts to simply live free and prosperous lives. They are tired of a government that abuses them, quite literally, every single day.

The liberty movement that has arisen in recent years, which rallied to support my presidential runs, helped get Rand elected to the U.S. Senate, and helped elect property rights and civil liberties champion Representative Justin Amash (R-MI) in the

House, represents a new force in politics. It is a force that recognizes that government's war on our liberties has long been a bipartisan effort. This is not simply about Republican versus Democrat, but about people who believe in the Constitution and individual rights versus the politicians in both parties who don't. This isn't about party, but about people who believe in limited government against those who seem to think it is unlimited.

This is about liberty versus tyranny.

Tea Party members are outraged by what our government has done to private property rights and how citizens are manhandled in our airports. Millions of young Americans flocked to my campaign rallies in the last four years to hear the message of liberty and how important it remains as they face an uncertain future. Countless independent voters and even some liberal Democrats are increasingly fearful of a government that continues to damage individual rights and civil liberties.

It is the rising generation that gives me hope that we can turn the tide. There are more needless and harmful government regulations today than at perhaps any other time in our history. There are also more Americans unwilling to sit idly by and take this abuse than ever before.

Rand has become one of the leading voices in the ongoing fight against our rogue regulatory state. No other U.S. senator in recent memory has done more to fight against the big-government politicians in both parties who consider the Bill of Rights little more than a list of suggestions. Thanks to Rand's leadership on these issues, some on Capitol Hill, and especially in the Republican Party, have began changing their minds in a more liberty-oriented direction. Thanks to my many wonderful supporters and the movement they've created, it looks like more liberty-minded leaders could soon be arriving in Washington, D.C., to join this fight than ever before.

The stories told in this book will horrify you. These stories are the reason Rand fights so hard to keep government off people's backs and out of their lives. These stories are why the message of liberty continues to ring louder and clearer than ever, as the statists learn that the harder they push, the harder the American people will push back.

When I first came to Congress in 1976, I did so because I believed the country was going down the wrong track. As bad as things were then, today it often seems like we've gone completely off track. The old saying that things must get worse before they can get better might be true, but the public outcry against a government that has truly gone mad—these horrible and atrocious government bullies—might be the final straw that helps restore constitutional government in our time.

Introduction

Ronald Reagan famously said, "The nine most terrifying words in the English language are, 'I'm from the government and I'm here to help.'" Three decades later, American life is micromanaged at every imaginable level. Citizens' basic day-to-day activities are subject to government scrutiny. We endure a federal government that has invaded virtually every aspect of our lives—from light bulbs, to toilets, to lemonade stands and beyond.

Our federal government regulates everything and anything. How much water goes into your commode. How much water comes out of your showerhead. The temperature of the water in your washing machine. How many miles to the gallon your car must get.

Americans' privacy is violated at every turn. Since the implementation of the Patriot Act, your banking records, your credit card account, your gun registration, and your phone bill have become easy pickings for government snoops, who can do pretty much anything they like with your personal information without the hassle of having to get a warrant. The government can literally break down your door, seize your property, and even seize you, based on rules and regulations created by unelected bureaucrats with zero accountability.

Congress has abdicated its constitutional role as the federal body that makes laws by allowing agencies like the EPA, FDA, USDA, and TSA to make their own laws through regulations and red tape. These agencies have assumed frightening new powers over the everyday lives of American citizens, giving these government entities free rein over you and me in ways unprecedented in our country's history.

Our ever-growing nanny state now includes an arsenal of unconstitutional and unprecedented surveillance and law enforcement powers. These government powers aren't exactly subtle in action or intent. Does anyone think a government with thirty-eight *armed* federal agencies is kidding around? They're not. They mean business.

Your business.

Everyone understands that some federal agents must be armed. But most Americans are surprised to learn that the Department of Agriculture, the Fish and Wildlife Service, and the Environmental Protection Agency all have armed SWAT teams. Why do such agencies need small armies to enforce, supposedly, mere fishing and hunting regulations? Why do we need to arm government bureaucrats to protect the environment?

The 1985 dystopian movie *Brazil* was a comedy about life under a totalitarian bureaucracy. In one scene, a man in full body armor with an automatic weapon is seen scaling a high-rise apartment building. Finally reaching a balcony, he climbs over the railing and knocks on the door. The voice inside the apartment asks, "Who is it?" The armed man answers, "The plumber."

In *Brazil*'s imaginary police state, the only way for this plumber to evade armed bureaucrats enforcing "regulations" was to arm himself.

American dystopia didn't come overnight. President Obama has introduced and implemented thousands of new regulations, many of which are needless and don't make any sense. But we can't blame President Obama for everything (though historians will allot him his fair share). The regulatory morass that now engulfs us came incrementally, accumulating over time to create the monstrosity we face today. Democrats and Republicans alike deserve blame.

Many Americans remember the now infamous mercury-laden Chinese-made $4 light bulbs that were mandated by Congress in 2007—a mandate by a *Republican* Congress and signed into law by a *Republican* president. In the name of energy efficiency, Congress decided to ban incandescent light bulbs, which are now supposed to be phased out completely by 2014.

But, as noted, the alternative to incandescent light bulbs isn't much better.

When I sharply questioned a Department of Energy bureaucrat about the light bulb mandate and consumer choice, my Democrat colleagues said that the ban on incandescent bulbs was beyond criticism because a bipartisan majority had passed it.

Beyond criticism? Government overreach doesn't become constitutional or morally right simply because both parties agree to it.

I began my questioning of the DOE bureaucrat by asking, "Are you pro-choice?" She hesitated and then responded, trying to be clever, "For light bulbs!" I told her that she was not pro-choice. I told her that she was only for consumer "choice" if Americans were forced to "choose" from a list of government-approved light bulbs.

The incandescent light bulb is no longer a choice—so decrees our government.

When a Fish and Wildlife SWAT team raided the Gibson Guitar Corporation in 2009, seizing millions in property and padlocking their warehouses, it was not under any authority given by President Obama, but President Bush. Republicans and Democrats had joined together in a bipartisan fashion to make it a crime to break foreign laws and regulations.

How did this happen in America?

Since becoming a United States senator, I have been inside the halls of power in Washington, D.C., fighting to change this alarming and tyrannical direction America seems to be taking. It amazes me how many Washington leaders either don't know or don't seem to care that these things are happening. They think that I'm being an alarmist, when I'm hearing horror stories from my constituents and others that should be cause for concern to all Americans. Often I can find allies willing to help, but much more often I find politicians who only want to stand in the way of any changes to the status quo. Meanwhile, too many American citizens find themselves harassed and abused by their government with no hope of recourse.

We have been asleep. Many of us have thought simply electing Republicans was enough to protect our privacy, property, and constitutional freedoms, but we failed to realize that it makes a significant difference what type of Republicans we elect.

Understanding how we've arrived at this point would be much simpler if we could just blame those bad ol' Democrats— but the story of regulatory overreach and abuse is unquestionably bipartisan. It is a story of congressional abdication of power, a Congress that allowed its rightful constitutional powers to be siphoned off by a runaway regulatory bureaucracy. This bureaucracy has become more powerful than any senator or congressman and in some instances even more powerful than the president.

The stories in this book will shock you. First-generation immigrants jailed for moving dirt on their own land. A nurse separated from her small child and sentenced to eighty-seven months in prison—also for moving dirt on her own land.

Though it might sound like it, these are not jokes.

Did an arrogant and armed "wetlands police" arrive with the election of President Obama? No, this rogue government agency's origins come from a seemingly responsible piece of legislation called the Clean Water Act. In 1989, President George H. W. Bush vowed that America would lose no "wetlands" under his watch (a vow he unfortunately kept better than his "no new taxes" pledge). Under the first President Bush, a government wetlands manual was created that essentially emboldened federal agents' power, allowing them to seek out and punish private property owners for doing nothing more than moving dry dirt on dry land. The federal government had—however erroneously, illogically, or nonsensically—defined these dry areas as "wetlands." It turns out that a wetlands is simply whatever an agency like the EPA says it is—no matter how many experts or even other government officials say to the contrary. In this book, you will read stories of property owners jailed for doing nothing more than committing the "crime" of moving dirt on their own property. Seriously.

Going after agencies like the EPA or being critical of ridiculous laws and regulations is enough to invite accusations that you somehow don't care about the environment. At the liberal website Think Progress, blogger Tonya Somanader wrote in 2011: "A steadfast enemy to the air he breathes, Sen. Rand

Paul (R-KY) is a never-ending source of attacks on environmental regulations and the EPA."

So there you have it. Because I "attack" government agencies, I must somehow be against the environment, say many
on the Left.

I consider myself a Crunchy-Con—that is, a conservative
who likes, enjoys, and wants to conserve the environment.

I compost. I built my composting bins from wood I sal-
vaged from my kids' old tree fort. I have a Giant Sequoia that
I planted and am trying to cultivate in my yard in Kentucky.
I have personally dug up and transplanted dozens of trees,
some of which are now over thirty feet tall. One tree that I'm
particularly proud of is a cherry tree that descends from the
cherry trees of the tidal basin adjacent to the Jefferson Memo-
rial, given to the United States by Japan's Emperor Hirohito
in the early 1900s.

I am a biker, a hiker, a rafter and a kayaker. I believe no one
has the right to pollute another person's property, and if it
occurs the polluter should be made to pay for cleanup and dam-
ages. I am not against all regulation. I am against overzealous
regulation. Nor am I against all government. I often joked on
the campaign trail that I was for $2.2 trillion worth of gov-
ernment—what we currently bring in in revenue—but certainly
not for the $3.8 trillion of government we currently spend.

Conservatives enjoy the environment as much as liberals. But conservatives differ from liberals in that we appreciate how industries restore and replenish the environment. We
conservatives understand that man uses the environment to
create the comforts of the modern world, and that regulations
require a balancing act between economic growth, jobs and
the environment.

The Clean Water Act, like many regulations, started out with good intentions. It prohibited dumping "pollutants" into the "navigable waters" of the United States. Who could argue against that? The problem arose when environment courts began defining dirt as a "pollutant" and plain old backyards as "navigable" streams.

Since at least the Great Depression, the courts have decided that pollution is to be controlled not by tort law and regional acceptance of norms, but through federal regulation. Some have argued that a robust tort law approach would actually have allowed less pollution or damage to the environment than a regulatory approach. This is not to say there should be no federal role—even strict originalist judges understand that the Constitution allows regulation of activities that can indirectly affect innocent third parties if the activity in question involves interstate commerce. No one is saying there should be no federal role in environmental regulation—only that there has been too much federal regulation, much of it to the detriment of the environment.

Often opponents want to depict the position of libertarians and conservatives on this issue as being uncaring about the environment, or the health consequences of pollution. Nothing could be farther from the truth. In fact, many limited-government advocates point to how government regulation often exempts big business or big agriculture. Many of these regulations actually benefit big business and punish the small businessman or farmer, most of whom can't afford lawyers to guide them through byzantine regulations and mountains of paperwork.

Author Joel Salatin is a sustainable farmer who writes frequently about how overregulation has hampered and damaged the small farmer. Salatin's belief in less regulation does not mean that he somehow accepts pollution. He simply advocates what many libertarians advocate: strict property rights and swift recourse if someone pollutes your land, your water, or your air.

In fact, it has been argued that a property-rights approach would have prevented the pollution of Lake Michigan, Boston Harbor, and other sites where municipalities either directly dumped sewage and other pollutants, or issued licenses to private business that allowed those businesses to pollute.

When I was interviewed by Comedy Central's Jon Stewart while promoting my first book *The Tea Party Goes to Washington*, Stewart asked me about pollution and government regulation. I replied that virtually all the evidence shows that levels of airborne and waterborne pollutants have been declining for decades. Stewart said, "But that's because of federal pollution regulations." I agreed, explaining that the point is not that we shouldn't advocate regulations, but that if the current regulations are working—why must we now make the regulations so severe that most business can't afford to comply?

In some cases, businesses cannot physically comply because the regulations make demands beyond the scientific methods that exist for compliance. This was the case when I fought against increasing the severity of the Clean Air Transport Act. The amount of sulfur dioxide and nitrous oxide allowed to be emitted had been lowered only a few years ago, and the four-decade trend for these emissions had been declining steadily. In fact, these byproducts of burning coal were at their lowest levels ever.

On the Senate floor, I showed my colleagues a picture of Pittsburgh, Pennsylvania, from the early twentieth century and then a picture of Pittsburgh today. The contrast was amazing. In the early 1900s, the street lanterns were often on at noon. A man's white shirt would blacken from the soot in the air. And now Pittsburgh's skyline gleams and sparkles. (Granted, some of these improvements might have something to do with the demise of the steel industry, but that's another story.)

Nevertheless, the obvious deduction is that pollution has been declining for the last hundred years or more. The peak of America's pollution problems were likely in the late 1800s, when not only did industry lack pollution controls but also many homes were often heated with coal.

This point is well made by John Stossel of Fox News, who in one of his television specials asks a fifth-grade class a simple question: Is the environment more polluted now or forty years ago? The overwhelming majority of kids raise their hands and answer without hesitation: "Now, of course."

Al Gore and the environmental zealots have co-opted the debate on these issues. The Left has successfully politicized any public discussions about the environment and regulation. Probably no single issue is more misrepresented and distorted on a regular basis than the environment.

Try arguing the facts, and instead of having a rational debate, your opponents will show you a movie of the Statue of Liberty submerged or polar bears drowning. Even the Senate floor is not immune from arguments based primarily on emotion and distortion of the truth. When I argued against regulation increases on cross-air transport, which deals with potential airborne pollutants crossing state lines, Barbara Boxer came to the floor with pictures of children with masks inhaling oxygen. She claimed that if we didn't accept the more stringent regulations 35,000 children would die. Really? She claimed that the increased incidents of asthma attacks were from pollutants. She personally blamed me and accused me of wanting to kill 35,000 children. I'm not kidding.

Try having an intelligent discussion with someone who is accusing you of supporting genocide. It's not possible.

I responded to Boxer that if the incidents of asthma attacks were rising and the levels of pollutants had been falling for decades, then these two things would be inversely proportional. In other words, decreasing pollution was correlated with increasing asthma attacks; or, put another way, increasing pollution would be correlated with lower asthma attacks. The truth of the matter is that the evidence points to no correlation. Objective scientists say that the cause of asthma is not yet fully understood.

The point is that when we allow arguments to degenerate into emotions and platitudes we lose track of two important things: 1. Are the current regulations actually working? 2. Will the new regulations mean loss of jobs?

Another issue that came up during my first session in the Senate was pipeline regulations. Eight people died in a terrible pipeline explosion in San Bruno, California, in 2010. Politicians in Washington are quick to jump at the first possible moment to "fix" aproblem. Then, of course, they take credit for fixing the problem. But these politicians often take action so hastily that they not only mistake identifying the actual problem, they cause other unintended problems in the process.

Groucho Marx understood it well when he said, "Politics is the art of looking everywhere for problems, finding them, misdiagnosing the problem and applying the wrong remedy. The pipeline issue fit this exact description. Senators Boxer and

Dianne Feinstein leaped at the opportunity to take legislative action after the San Bruno tragedy, to show their constituents that they cared. These senators presented a series of regulatory reforms for pipelines.

Boxer and Feinstein wanted to pass their bill by unanimous consent, which means there is no floor debate and no amendment attached or considered—and, more times than not, nobody actually reads the bill. I put a hold on their bill. It could not pass without the unanimous consent of all hundred senators, which I was not willing to give. How did Senators Boxer and Feinstein respond? Did they attempt to contact my office or call me to ask what my objections were? Did they try to even see if I had any legitimate reason for concern? Hell no—they called a reporter instead and proceeded to read me the riot act in the press. They attempted to portray me as someone who was uncaring and not serious about addressing this problem.

I was not amused. I was also not about to take their abuse lying down. We responded that we were holding the bill for two reasons: First, the accident report on the San Bruno explosion was due to come out the following week. Wouldn't it be reasonable to actually read the accident report and consider it before deciding on sweeping reforms? And second, Feinstein and Boxer's bill grandfathered in old pipelines—this meant that old pipelines would be exempt from the new rules! This meant that the over fifty-year-old San Bruno pipeline itself, where the fatal tragedy had occurred, would be exempt from the new rules these senators wanted to impose.

Something seemed fishy here.

In Washington, bills are often touted publicly to placate a certain part of the electorate or a particular politician's voter base, but on closer examination you'll find that nothing is actually done to really fix any problems. Sometimes this occurs intentionally, and sometimes it occurs unintentionally simply because everyone is in such a rush.

The more my staff and I examined Boxer and Feinstein's bill, the more we were concerned that it would not fix the problem, and that the victims of the San Bruno explosion and their families would be tricked into thinking that Washington had actually done something positive or preventive—that politicians somehow were atoning for this tragedy by enacting better regulations.

As we investigated, we discovered that not only were older pipelines being exempted from the new regulations, but also that this was not the first time this problem had been papered over.

In 1985, the National Transportation Safety Board's Office of Pipeline Safety reported on two explosions in Kentucky where deaths occurred. The report specifically stated that one much needed reform was to end the exemption of older pipelines from standard regulations. This reform never happened, and twenty-six years later, Boxer and Feinstein's legislation would have simply papered over the problem again.

I said "No way!" During my Senate campaign, I had promised to read bills before voting on them, and that I would not be a rubber stamp for well-intentioned but ultimately meaningless reforms. We won this battle and my staff was able to include a requirement for testing of the older pipelines. Just weeks later, this test discovered another faulty part, in a different section, of the San Bruno pipeline that had previously exploded.

If I had not opposed Boxer and Feinstein's unanimous consent vote, read the bill, investigated the problem, and helped institute this testing, the problematic part of the pipeline could have feasibly gone undetected. There is always a greater danger in Washington, D.C., of politicians acting hastily without thinking, than in debating and contemplating any new rules and regulations.

As the stories of regulatory abuse unfold in the following pages, don't be fooled by those on the Left who demonize me as someone who believes in no government regulations. My argument is that regulations need to be reasonable and economically practical. My point is that the obvious need for safety and pollution control should, and can, be balanced with a need for job creation and economic growth.

What scares most businessmen and women is that the Obama administration has gotten out of control, with environmental extremists running amok. In 2010, EPA administrator Al Armendariz reinforced this notion when he described at a public event how he viewed regulation enforcement: "It was kind of like how the Romans used to, you know, conquer villages in the Mediterranean.... They'd go into a little Turkish town somewhere, they'd find the first five guys they saw, and they'd crucify them." Armendariz added, "You make examples out of people who are, in this case, not complying with the law...and you hit them as hard as you can."

Luckily, Armendariz was forced to resign, but as long as zealots like this are allowed to run our monstrous regulatory bureaucracies, America's growth and progress is endangered. We need a reassessment of whether current regulations are actually working; and regarding any new regulations, we must take into account what their effect will be on job creation. Then, and only then, will we begin to thrive as a country again.

It's amazing the many ways in which our federal government is now completely out of control. It's maddening how oppressive and intrusive everyday life has become for millions of Americans who are just trying to go about their lives and be happy.

I found out on a recent trip just how long and invasive the tentacles of our federal government have become. I was flying out of Nashville back to Washington, D.C., where I was scheduled to speak to over 200,000 people—the largest crowd of my career—at the March for Life. But the TSA had other ideas. After I had removed my belt, my glasses, my wallet, and my shoes, the scanner and TSA still demanded something else— my dignity. I refused. After they told me that the scanner had detected something unusual near my leg, I offered to show them my leg. They were not interested. They wanted to pat me down. They wanted to touch me. I asked to be rescanned. They refused. I was detained in a ten-foot-square cubicle designed for potential terrorists. I explained to the TSA agents that I was a frequent flyer, and that just days prior I was allowed to be rescanned when the scanner had made an error.

At no time did I ask for special treatment, though I did insist that I, like all travelers, should be shown common courtesy. I was repeatedly instructed not to leave the cubicle. When I used my mobile phone to have my office start researching why the TSA would not simply rescreen me, I was threatened. The TSA agents told me that I would now be subjected to full-body patdown. I asked if I could simply start the screening process to show that the screener had made an error. I was told no, that once the process had been started and I had used my phone to call for help, I must now submit to a patdown or simply not fly. I thought to myself, "Have the terrorists won?" Have we sacrificed our liberty and our dignity for a false security?

Finally, the head of the Nashville airport TSA arrived—after I had missed my flight. He seemed inclined to let me be rescreened. Interestingly, the scanner did not go off the second time through. The TSA agents who had just given me the third degree said that some of the alarms are simply random. I was befuddled. So this agent was saying, admitting even, that passengers who do everything right—remove their belts, their wallets, their shoes, their glasses, and all the contents of their pockets—can still be stopped and forced to undergo a pat-down *randomly*? Travelers are tricked into believing the scanner actually detected something, *by design*?

I had been through some of this regulation nonsense before with TSA chief administrator John Pistole. In the spring of 2011, a six-year-old girl from my hometown of Bowling Green, Kentucky, was subjected to an invasive search despite her parents' objections. Pistole claimed that small children were indeed a risk because a girl in Kandahar, Afghanistan, had exploded a bomb in a market there. But Director Pistole, I said—this girl wasn't from Kandahar. She wasn't in Afghanistan. Isn't there a significant difference? Pistole explained in writing that the TSA had concluded that because a child in a market in Afghanistan exploded a bomb, all American children needed to be evaluated as potential threats. My response was that if you treat everyone equally as a potential threat then you direct most of your attention to those who are never going to attack us. Consequently, less time is spent focusing on those whose profiles indicate higher risk and a need for advanced screening.

Random screening not based on a risk assessment misdirects

the screening process and adds to the indignity of travel. It takes time away from screening the guy who has been to Yemen twice and regularly chats with known terrorists. Passengers who suffer through the process of partially disrobing should be rewarded with a less invasive examination. After that Nashville trip, I met with Congressman Jason Chaffetz and Darrell Issa. Issa is chairman of the House committee that oversees the TSA, and he is known as a public servant unafraid to challenge regulatory overreach. Together, we coauthored an Air Travelers' Bill of Rights to define and protect the dignity and privacy of air travelers.

Some days I fear that the regulators have won and the bullying bureaucrats already control our government. Yet after my ordeal with the TSA, members from both sides of the aisle came to me and said we must fix the TSA, that we must rein in the agency's arrogance. But even in the face of significant and bipartisan support to put limits on the TSA's power, the desired change remains elusive. The machinery of the bureaucracy, its inertness, its imponderable weight, has to date still defeated our best efforts of reform.

As you read these stories of everyday Americans bullied and badgered by their own government, I hope you get mad. More important, I hope you get inspired to channel your outrage into activism and involvement. In my first speech while I was still contemplating running for office, I repeated Sam Adams's exhortation that it does not require a majority to prevail, but rather an irate and tireless minority keen to set brushfires in people's minds.

This book speaks to that minority who've been victims of government abuse. It speaks to the irate and tireless, yet often powerless. It is meant to set brushfires in the minds of all Americans about what their government is really up to, whether behind their backs or in front of their faces.

Our Founders envisioned an America in which citizens would bully the government, not the other way around. This book is my effort to bring that America back.

PART 1

* * *

Property Wrongs—EPA Bullies

"No person shall be...deprived of life, liberty, or property, without due process of law; nor shall private property be taken for public use without just compensation..."

—United States Constitution, Amendment V

1

★ ★ ★

Government "Wetland" Goons

"The true foundation of republican government is the equal right of every citizen in his person and property and in their management."
—THOMAS JEFFERSON

                              ★ ★ ★

As a U.S. senator, it is my job is to keep an eye on what our government is up to. As a conservative, I have grave concern that our government has become completely out of control. This is true in ways that even many of my fellow conservatives don't realize in the immediate sense. Many elected officials don't realize it. Many Americans don't realize it, which I'm quite sure is completely fine with many elected officials.

But what our government is doing is not "fine." It's infuriating.

Since its creation in 1970, the Environmental Protection Agency has done more harm than good. Typical of government as opposed to private solutions, with the inception of the EPA bad policy began to outweigh the good intentions, the massive cost quickly surpassed the original concern of "doing nothing," and the new powers given to Washington bureaucrats inevitably began to corrupt absolutely. If the race of government bullying were a contest between different agencies, the EPA would take the crown.

EPA regulations cost more than 5 percent of our annual gross domestic product (which was over $15 trillion in 2012). This is equivalent to the costs of defense and homeland security combined. Most Americans are unaware of this. Assuming that the EPA is somehow just protecting the environment, as the name would suggest, too many Americans are unaware that it and agencies like it are yet more representatives of the bloated bureaucracy that characterizes every other part of our federal government.

Whether by coincidence or design, since EPA regulations began taking property, jobs, and businesses away from citizens, unemployment in America has increased by 33 percent. This abuse of power by the implementation of regulations infringes upon all Americans' basic rights, whether or not some of us are ever directly affected by their rules.

Too often our rights are violated by abusive and power-hungry EPA bureaucrats who use threats, coercion, and force to implement power grabs. I wish these instances of abuse were random and the exception, but they have unfortunately come to characterize what many Americans now rightly see as a rogue government agency. EPA regulations have hampered landowners' ability to manage their private property as they please and have seriously impaired job creation. As with the massive cost of the EPA, many Americans are unaware of the routine suffering caused by the overreach of such regulatory agencies.

One of the most egregious examples of the overreach of government is in the enforcement of federal wetlands regulations (*see* http://water.epa.gov/lawsregs/guidance/wetlands/sec404.cfm).

Wetlands are a creation of the Clean Water Act of 1972, though interestingly, what qualifies as a wetland is ill-defined, to say the least. In fact, the definition is so nebulous that as recently as 2011 the EPA was still issuing guidelines about wetlands regulations. What constitutes a wetland is almost impossible to discern for individuals, and even when they believe their property is not a wetland, the EPA can declare it so according to no definition but their own. Property owners are not subject to simple rule of law, but rather are constantly at the mercy of a government agency that makes its own laws, often without rhyme, reason, common sense, or oversight.

This lack of specificity in wetland law, sometimes intentional and sometimes through sloppiness, is indicative of a problem with Congress, whose initial flawed attempt at legislation—and repeated bungled attempts at oversight—have left the executive branch with far too much power to essentially fill in the blanks of legislation. Famously, the passage of Obamacare offers an example, where hundreds of times throughout the legislation actions are to be taken "by the director of HHS" (Health and Human Services) rather than at the direction of those who wrote the law in the first place.

When power is left in the hands of the executive, it will *always* grow. There is no mechanism to stop it within the executive branch. Budgets will balloon. Pages of regulations will sprout. And power will cause those in charge to act like masters instead of servants—something that happens all too frequently in our government these days.

Throughout this section the stories of those who have come forward to fight back against unimaginable abuse at the hands of government bullies will be told, sometimes in my words, when possible in their own words. I want you to know the details, the pain, the suffering. I want all Americans to know about the omnipresent harassment by the government in the lives of these ordinary, law-abiding citizens. It is entirely possible that you could be next.

In Pennsylvania, take the story of John Pozsgai, an immigrant from Hungary who worked as a mechanic and eventually saved enough money to purchase the land bordering his home in Morrisville, Pennsylvania. This land was nothing more than an old auto junkyard, and Mr. Pozsgai—simply taking pride in his home—proceeded to clean it up by removing seven thousand old tires and rusted-out automobiles. However, the EPA did not view this effort as a necessary, much less praiseworthy, cleanup, but rather as a violation of the Clean Water Act. You see, Mr. Pozsgai's property was deemed a "wetland," ambiguously defined by the EPA as any property that has some sort of connection to another wetland. That connection to a wetland was a small drainage ditch located on the edge of his property.

Mr. Pozsgai did not need a permit to dump topsoil on an isolated wetland. However, the Army Corps of Engineers insisted he apply for one. Next, the EPA set up surveillance cameras to capture Mr. Pozsgai filling his land with topsoil. EPA agents then arrested him for "discharging pollutants into waters of the United States." These "pollutants" consisted of earth, topsoil, and sand. The EPA openly admits that no hazardous wastes were involved in the case, yet Mr. Pozsgai was found guilty and sentenced to three years in prison and fined $202,000. Mr. Pozsgai spent one and a half years in prison, one and a half in a halfway house, and was under supervised probation for five years. His family went bankrupt and was unable to pay its property taxes on the land. This happened to a man who fled communism who came to America seeking freedom and prosperity.

A similar breach of power can be studied in the case of John Rapanos. Federal officials prosecuted Mr. Rapanos for shoveling dirt around on his property in Bay County, Michigan. The EPA and Army Corps of Engineers filed charges against him for "polluting" the wetlands by leveling the soil on his property. Under the "migratory molecule" rule, the Army

Corps claims that any isolated wetland can fall under federal jurisdiction because there is a speculative possibility that a water molecule from one wetland may reach another navigable waterway. In Mr. Rapanos's case, the nearest navigable water is roughly twenty miles from his property.

Federal officials had little real evidence against Mr. Rapanos, and U.S. district judge Lawrence Zatkoff threw out the conviction, refusing to follow the unjust federal guidelines enforced by the EPA. Unfortunately, Judge Zatkoff was over-ruled by the U.S. Court of Appeals for the Sixth Circuit. Mr. Rapanos later appealed his conviction to the U.S. Supreme Court, yet the Court refused to hear his case. He now faces possible jail time.

Mr. and Mrs. Michael Sackett of Priest Lake, Idaho, have also fallen victim to the EPA's abusive and overbearing practices. The Sacketts sought to build a house on their half acre of land, yet after construction broke ground the EPA interfered, claiming the family had violated the Clean Water Act by placing fill materials into "wetlands." Like others targeted by the EPA, the Sacketts' property was designated a wetland. Yet their neighbors had built houses on either side of their lot, and the Sacketts' lot already had established sewage lines. Their lot does not harbor a lake, pond, or stream, yet the EPA is requiring them to obtain a building permit that would cost more than the value of their land. The Sacketts proceeded by filing suit, but the request was dismissed by a federal judge. But in March of 2012 the Supreme Court overruled the lower court, which allowed the Sacketts to move forward with a civil action under the Administrative Procedure Act. This act, as Supreme Court Justice Antonin Scalia explained in writing the unanimous decision, provides for judicial review of "final agency action for which there is no other adequate remedy in court." The Supreme Court is now considering these violations.

The repeated abuse of power by the EPA has been noted across the country and it infringes on the lives of all Americans. You will hear the stories above, along with those of Robbie Rigley, Ocie Mills, and Bill Ellen. You'll hear about the harassment of people like Mark Groenendyk and Marinus Van Leuzen.

One of the few bright spots is that some of these folks above, and others like them, were helped by good men and women who have devoted their life to helping fight these tyrannical government abuses. The Pacific Legal Foundation, which is currently before the Supreme Court representing the Sacketts on their case, and has dozens of similar cases around the country, helps lead this effort. I want to tell their story also, because ultimately this book is about how we can fix the problem and the examples of hope given by those fighting and winning today.

Property rights were once regarded as fundamental to the protection of liberty, and it is time that legislators restore the value of personal property and rein in government overreach. At the end of this section, I'll tell you exactly what I want to do about the problems exemplified in these stories.

On February 7, 2011, I introduced the REINS Act (Regulations from the Executive in Need of Scrutiny Act). This act requires that all major regulations—those greater than $100 million—be voted on by Congress. Opening the regulatory process to public scrutiny will make government agencies accountable to all American citizens. This is a commonsense reform that will increase congressional liability, improve the regulatory process, and protect citizens from restrictions being placed on their economic and private practices. The REINS Act ensures that federal agencies cannot destroy jobs, our economy, or our way of life by implementing unnecessary regulations. These harmful and abusive regulations must end in order to safeguard the American freedom we all recognize as our birthright.

On February 16, 2012, I introduced the Defense of the Environment and Property Act, which would finally define wetlands and navigable waters in the law and stop the out-of-control EPA in its war on private property.

Together, bills like these would send the agency and rules that led to the inexcusable abuse of John Pozsgai and others whose lives have been ruined to the ash heap of history—where they belong.

2

★ ★ ★

Escaping Communism and Finding Tyranny in America

"While my father was still able to speak, I asked him, 'Daddy, what should we do with the land?' He muttered in broken words, 'Build a hospital to fix people like me.'"

—Victoria Pozsgai-Khoury

* * *

October 12, 2011, Washington, D.C.: Victoria Pozsgai-Khoury appeared before a panel of U.S. senators for a roundtable discussion I hosted entitled "Property Wrongs." I led this discussion and invited Victoria to share her father's story—a story of the American dream gone astray because of power-grabbing bureaucrats and an overreaching, unjust government. Her father, Pennsylvania resident John Pozsgai, spent decades entangled in a legal battle with the EPA simply because he moved landfill from one area of his property to another.

Beginning in 1990, this legal battle with the EPA consumed and engulfed the Pozsgai family's lives for over twenty years.

When I originally asked Victoria to come to Washington to tell her family's story, she was very hesitant to attend due to her father's ailing condition. But John Pozsgai had spent his life fighting for and searching for true freedom—beginning with his escape from communism nearly fifty years ago.

Now, at age seventy-nine and in extremely poor health, he nevertheless urged his daughter to attend the Senate hearings and encouraged her to share with the nation their family's story of government abuse. To Mr. Pozsgai, getting his story heard was more important than having her present, kneeling and praying at what would unfortunately soon become his deathbed.

He was surrounded by many loved ones as he died, but his daughter Victoria was not there. Instead, she was carrying out his last wishes, speaking on her father's behalf to warn the nation of the constant abuse our government practices—abuses of power so serious that they will strip away everything you have and ruin your opportunity to prosper in our free nation.

While her father was dying, Victoria was telling the story of her family's rights, which were unjustly violated by tyrannical and cruel government bureaucrats. She was also telling the story of a remarkable life, one that epitomized what America is supposed to stand for—but a life faced with unimaginable struggles due to what, sadly, America has too often become.

Before coming to the United States fifty years ago, John Pozsgai fought communism. In the nation of his birth, Hungary, the Soviet regime conscripted him into their army and forced him to serve for his "motherland." He had no right to refuse this or any other dictate of his authoritarian government, yet refuse he did. In 1956, the Soviet army invaded Hungary. John Pozsgai refused to fight against his own countrymen and instead joined the resistance. But the Hungarian freedom fighters proved no match for Soviet tanks and the overall might of their authoritarian invaders, and John was forced to flee Hungary. He came to America, as millions of others seeking freedom have done.

John Pozsgai, like so many first-generation immigrants who escaped communism and government turmoil, loved America as much if not more than any native-born American. He knew what kind of precious and unique freedom he had found in this country, largely because he knew the tyranny he had left behind. John and Gizella Pozsgai came to America as refugees seeking freedom with nothing more than the clothes on their backs and virtually no English-language skills. Still, they worked together tirelessly and joyfully, building a family truck repair business in a garage behind their small home in Morrisville, Pennsylvania.

John Pozsgai worked hard in his new country. He paid taxes. He raised a family. He started his own business. He actively pursued the American dream and became a citizen of the United States.

Yet how did his adopted country treat him? Armed agents of the federal government arrested, tried, and imprisoned him for the environmental crime of placing fill clean dirt onto dry land. *His* dry land. Land that *he* bought and land that *he* owned. This freedom fighter bravely risked his life and escaped communism, only to be imprisoned by bureaucratic rules turned into crimes. These rules were written not by elected representatives, but by unelected appointees.

How could this happen in America? How could a country famous for freedom and the "rule of law" allow people to be imprisoned for moving dirt on their own property? The story of John Pozsgai and how he was sentenced to the bureaucratic gulag is one that needs to be told, and retold, and shouted from the highest rooftop!

Imprisoning people for running afoul of bureaucratic red tape is not an America to be proud of. It is not the America our Founding Fathers envisioned or desired. It is not the America to which generations of immigrants came to find freedom. It is not the America brave patriots fought and died to found. The bureaucrats who unjustly prosecute innocent individuals are truly disgraceful and their laws must be repealed. This is not some fanciful initiative—it is a moral imperative if a free America is to survive.

On December 30, 1988, John Pozsgai was found guilty on forty counts of violating the Clean Water Act. He was given the maximum fine of $202,000 and the maximum sentence of three years in prison, the longest jail term in history at the time for any environmental crime. To put this in perspective, Pozsgai received a harsher punishment than those at Exxon responsible for the *Exxon Valdez* oil spill. Based on his punishment at the time of his conviction, Mr. Pozsgai was the worst polluter in the history of the United States.

So what heinous crime did John Pozsgai commit? What horrible toxin had he unleashed? How many deaths had he caused?

Pozsgai was charged with "discharging pollutants into the navigable waters of the United States." That sounds terrible. None of us want pollutants in our streams, lakes, and rivers. What toxic, life-threatening chemical did this alleged monster dump into our waters?

The answer is nothing. According to court documents, no chemical, toxins, or trash were ever dumped into any stream or river by John Pozsgai. The "pollutant" Pozsgai was accused of discharging was dirt—clay and mud—the same "harmful" dirt we all made mud pies with as young children.

You are probably thinking I am kidding, right? Dirt?

Yes, Pozsgai was convicted of discharging dirt. But surely the dirt must have clogged a stream and created a mess? Surely his actions harmed his neighbors and the environmental well-being of his community? His actions had to hurt someone or something, right? Well, no. The dirt was fill and it was literally scooped up and moved from one end of the property to the other end of the property. The dirt was discharged from one piece of his dry land onto another piece of his dry land. That's it. No more, no less. Which begs the obvious question: How can the federal government claim dry ground is a "navigable" water?

Herein lies the crux of the bureaucratic and regulatory labyrinth that is Washington. Congress passed a law that forbids the discharge of pollutants into bodies of navigable water. Unelected bureaucrats and administrative judges altered that law to make pollutants include dirt and to interpret "navigable waters" to mean low-lying ground that may have had water in it at some point, or has plants growing on it that can also grow in wet conditions.

How could this happen? How could we imprison people for crimes that only became crimes when bureaucrats doctored laws to make them mean something Congress never intended them to mean? And how did "navigable waters" come to include any low-lying, moist ground?

One of the main culprits is the ever-elastic definition of "wetlands."

We have all heard that term. Most of us logically assume it is used to describe large, environmentally sensitive areas like the Everglades or the Gulf coast. But this is not always the case. This is often not the case. Unfortunately, law-abiding citizens like Mr. Pozsgai had to learn this the hard way.

Interestingly, the Clean Water Act never even mentioned the term "wetlands" while passing through Congress for approval. The unelected bureaucracy simply created the concept and defines it in distinct terminology dependent upon whatever scenario they are currently considering. "Wetlands" quite literally can mean whatever the EPA wants it to mean.

The definition of wetlands has become so absurd and transparent that the Army Corps of Engineers developed the "migratory bird theory." This theory states that if your land is a stopping point for any migratory bird that has traveled between real navigable waters, then your land is now de facto connected to the interstate navigable streams. I'm not kidding.

This theory is irrational and completely illogical. How did it ever become enforceable law? It happened because Congress has abdicated its duty in this area, just as it has been so derelict in countless other constitutional duties. Congress wrote vague yet sweeping laws that allowed regulatory breaches to become crimes even if the person had no intent of committing a crime. Citizens often run afoul of these rules inadvertently due to the constant evolution of complex and unexplained regulations.

What was not a crime in 1974 became a crime in 1975 when the courts defined pollutants to include dirt. What was not a crime in 1987 became a crime in 1989 when President George H. W. Bush rewrote the wetlands policy to double the amount of private land covered, to essentially place an assertion of 100 million acres of land under the purview of an unelected, unrestrained, and unpredictable "wetlands police."

The injustice of unelected bureaucrats creating their own laws and sending American citizens to prison is as egregious as it is hard to believe. I can guarantee you that John Pozsgai and his family could not, and still cannot, believe it. Neither can the Sackett family, nor could the Wrigley family. Nor could the various other individuals who've been abused by overreaching bureaucracy. Their stories are the tales of freedom fighters. They are bravely fighting this outrageous government abuse and looking for permanent solutions so that no other American has to go through what they did. Their stories are real. They are frightening.

John Pozsgai's battle with the EPA and Army Corps of Engineers began in 1986 when he purchased a dump located near his home. Remember throughout Pozsgai's story that we are indeed just talking about a dump—just what you would imagine, with old tires, junk, and debris strewn everywhere. The dump was a complete eyesore and had been for over thirty years. This wasn't a lake. It wasn't a beach. It wasn't a riverfront. It was a dump. Nothing more, nothing less.

The Pozsgais purchased the lot with the intention of expanding the family business by building a large shop for truck repairs. He sought and received all of the proper local permits from the Department of Labor and the local Department of Environmental Protection.

Mr. Pozsgai had a plan that would both clean up a thirty-year eyesore—a worthless piece of property—as well as create more jobs in his hometown. One would think this sounds like exactly the kind of thing any government would be promoting and encouraging. It sounds like exactly the kind of property stewardship and community contribution most Americans would praise, right?

But this isn't what happened.

The Pennsylvania Department of Environmental Protection gave the Pozsgais the go-ahead, including stating that their property was not on the National Wetlands Inventory map. Even if there were any wetlands, additional fill was pre-authorized by the Corps under Nationwide Permit No. 26 for up to ten acres for isolated wetlands. The Pozsgais felt assured that there would be no problems and no holdups from the government.

After this state evaluation, John Pozsgai mortgaged his house to buy the property and began to clean up and clear the site for construction.

But instead of Pozsgai being commended by the community for his backbreaking efforts, on August 24, 1988, the Corps of Engineers and EPA sued him in federal civil court for allowing clean, nontoxic fill material to be placed on less than three-quarters of an acre on the so-called wetland area of the property.

It was clear that these federal thugs had a vendetta: In fact, the government had been conducting aerial surveillance of the property since Pozsgai's renovations began. They even planted a video camera in a neighbor's house to further videotape Mr. Pozsgai's property.

Why did our government do this? There was no legitimate reason for Mr. Pozsgai to be targeted. It was an injustice and an outrage, clear and simple.

And it didn't stop there.

Just a few days later, the U.S. attorney in Philadelphia had several federal agents surround Pozsgai in his shop and arrested him. He was handcuffed and hauled off to federal criminal court in Philadelphia. He wasn't even allowed a phone call. Mrs. Pozsgai sat weeping, saying it was just like when the Soviets came into Hungary and took family and neighbors without any justification.

The Pozsgais were eventually told that the EPA had made a criminal case against them. Yet in the meantime the family bailed their father out of jail and began preparing for what was to come—an attack by the federal government on their father's most basic rights.

After posting bail and returning home, the family found two armed agents searching their house and business for illegal firearms. Victoria Pozsgai-Khoury described the scene, saying, "It was like watching thieves burglarize your home and not being able to do anything. We felt violated for years after this experience." The EPA officials never found any firearms—because they did not exist. Claims to the contrary by these government thugs were just as bogus as their wetlands claims had been.

In their arguments, the Corps and the EPA spun a tale of federally regulated wetlands on this isolated property because it was adjacent to a drainage ditch that somehow connected underground to the nonnavigable Delaware Canal. They switched maps and locations or simply misread them, and misdirected the officials to the wrong coordinates. They lacked correct elevations, they falsified forensic soil data, and they lacked soil DNA—soil diatoms and anaerobes. They manufactured a phony wetlands delineation lacking proper photogrammetric aerials. Adding to this delusion and confusion, these agencies couldn't even agree on a clear definition of what "wetlands" were or where they existed on Mr. Pozsgai's property. It appears as though the only thing they could agree on was the target—they had their sights set on John Pozsgai and they were going to take him down regardless.

The EPA and prosecution had somehow contrived a drainage ditch to be a stream and then marked it as such on aerial photos that were later submitted in court. The stormwater drainage ditch was filled with over seven thousand old tires, which Mr. Pozsgai painstakingly removed at his own cost. The debris and tires in that drainage ditch caused regular flooding on Bridge Street, which affected the Pozsgais' basement as well as some of the neighboring properties. After the property was cleaned up there were no more floods. In fact, no flooding was reported on that property for the next twenty-five years, even with three epic floods taking place in surrounding areas.

The drainage ditch in question borders Pozsgai's property and was created by the DOT prior to 1936. Even going through property deeds dating as far back as the 1800s, no wetlands were ever found on this particular site.

At every juncture throughout this ordeal the Pozsgais kept asking, "How can we make this work? What do we have to do to have rights on our own land?" They knew this situation was a terrible misunderstanding. The prosecution had wrong addresses, wrong site maps, wrong elevations/topography, wrong slopes, and wrong soil samples that were all contributing factors to the Pozsgais' dilemma. It turned out Morrisville has two streets with the same name, and these agencies kept mistaking one for the other. This would cause massive confusion in the courtroom.

On December 30, 1988, the court reached a verdict—John Pozsgai was found guilty on forty counts of violating the Clean Water Act. Why? Again, all he'd done was "damage" a few acres of so-called federal wetlands by using clean, non-toxic, nonhazardous fill. He was given the maximum fine of $202,000 and the maximum sentence of three years in prison. As I mentioned earlier, this was the longest jail term in history at that time for *any* environmental crime, even more than for the *Exxon Valdez* oil spill or for dumping hazardous waste in lakes.

The day after Thanksgiving in 1990, John Pozsgai began

serving his sentence in Allenwood federal prison, about a 400-mile round trip from his home and family. By July of the following year the Pozsgai family was bankrupt.

Where once he was a very productive citizen who paid taxes on his land, he was now a ward of the state and unable to produce anything because of the injustices visited upon him by his own government.

Pozsgai ended up serving a year and a half of hard time; he spent another year and a half in a halfway house and was given five years' supervised probation. His fine was later reduced to $5,000 thanks to another appeal by their attorney, Paul Kamenar. Mr. Kamenar successfully argued that the fine was excessive due to the Pozsgais' meager finances and negative net worth.

During Pozsgai's incarceration, the government ordered a "restoration." They dug up more than ten acres of the fourteen-acre site. They moved and removed twice as much as Pozsgai's said violation, and continued digging pits and ditches all over the site. A huge hole was dug, which EPA officials said would become a wetlands pond. Ten years later the hole remained high and dry. In 2000, nearly two decades after this ordeal began and not satisfied with the dry plot of land, the government forcibly dug up another area, blocking drainage from the site.

Now they finally have their pond.

As recently as 2007, the EPA was still harassing the Pozsgais. A federal judge sided with the EPA to say the Pozsgais were in contempt of an EPA order and must return their land to its previous status as a wetland. Does this mean the EPA and that federal judge want the Pozsgais to redump the thousands of old tires in the drainage ditch, and return the old rusted junk they cleared out?

None of this makes any sense.

After all of the government's intervention and abuse, not one dollar was paid to the Pozsgais for the loss and destruction of their land.

It's as though these government agencies went out of their way to ensure the financial and emotional suffering of the Pozsgai family. For example, they chased away the communications company Sprint, which wanted to build a cell phone tower on the land. Sprint evaluated the site and said the Pozsgai property had "no wetlands." They did soil borings over 150 feet deep. The judge said the tower should be permitted, but by the time the Corps took the Pozsgais to court, Sprint had found another site and the family lost yet another source of income.

There is literally no end to the countless tragic ways in which our federal government has cost the Pozsgai family.

On October 6, 2000, the Pozsgais were asked to testify before the House Committee on Government Reform, chaired by Congressman Dan Burton. John Pozsgai got a standing ovation and was given an apology by the chairman on behalf of the government. However, the local Corps did not show a kind face; instead, they continued their agenda and sued the family yet again. The agency then dug up their land to try once more to create a nonviable wetland pond out of an exempted storm drainage ditch.

Currently, the Pozsgais are in legal limbo—they can only use their site for permitted parking, severely limiting their income, with barely enough to pay property taxes.

This is madness.

Bureaucratic agencies like the EPA have proven themselves to be highly corrupt, choking out all efforts by small business to grow or expand. This has been going on for three decades and is no small part of our current economic depression. These agencies must become unaccountable to the American people and to Congress. They have instead become self-serving autocratic rulers, lording over any property owner they set their sights on. These rogue agencies bleed our economy and citizens dry. The Pozsgais came to this country for freedom. What they got instead was abuse. No American should ever have to go through what they experienced. Ever.

Mr. Pozsgai has since passed away. However, while her father was still able to speak, his daughter Victoria asked him, "Daddy, what should we do with the land?" He muttered in broken words, "Build a hospital and fix people like me." So that is what they plan to do. They want to partner with Alzheimer's and autism research groups around the country to build a learning and living facility on their property—paying tribute to their father, while trying to heal from their exhausting fight.

But sadly, the same restrictions on development are still there.

These out-of-control agencies—our own federal government—turned the Pozsgais' American dream into a nightmare. I feel it is my responsibility as a United States senator to make certain that no American will ever be stripped of their rights due to unlawful and despicable government overreach. My goal is to insist on implementing the necessary legislation to rein in these rogue government agencies and to stop tragedies like this from ever happening again.

3

★ ★ ★

From American Dream to Nightmare

"As a man is said to have a right to his property, he may be equally said to have a property in his rights."

—JAMES MADISON

In the northernmost reaches of the panhandle of Idaho you will find Priest Lake, a quaint and quiet home to more than forty thousand people. Mike and Chantell Sackett were hoping to join this community and make Priest Lake their home. Mike Sackett had dreamed of building a house on this beautiful lake ever since he camped there with friends as a high school student.

When he returned from his camping trip, Mike told his mother in no uncertain terms, "I am going to live on Priest Lake when I am older." She laughed off her son's grand declaration, at which point he reassured her, "Mark my words, I will build my home on that lake."

Chantell Sackett also had a special place in her heart for Priest Lake. Growing up, she spent her summers there. Chantell explains, "In the summertime, there is no other place you'd rather be. It's so peaceful and calm and pristine." So in 2007 the couple bought a piece of landlocked property in a preexisting subdivision on Priest Lake for $23,000. It appeared as though their American dream was coming true. They were finally going to become homeowners on the property they both grew up fantasizing about. "This was where we were going to live for our entire lives as far as we were concerned. This was going to be our *home* home," Chantell said.

The Sacketts owned a small construction company and were therefore very informed about the building permit process in the area. They applied for and received the proper local permits for their project, as they had done countless times in the past. For the Sacketts, this was routine. It was business as usual. Yet once they began preparing their land for construction, simply adding gravel and landfill, the EPA decided to get involved. The EPA showed up out of the blue and ordered them to stop working. The representatives did not have any particular credentials, nor did they have anything in writing charging the Sacketts with any violation. They were unwilling to explain why the Sacketts could not build their dream home on land that they owned.

The agency later claimed that the family had violated the Clean Water Act by placing fill materials onto wetlands. But this did not make sense. Their property was completely landlocked in a preexisting subdivision. So when the agents appeared on their land and ordered them to cease construction, Chantell Sackett went looking for an explanation.

She describes her conversation with the EPA: "I asked them if they had anything in writing. They said no. I asked if they had a stop-work order or anything. They said no. I asked if they had any proof or documentation saying that our property was a wetland. They said no, they didn't need any of that."

There is even an EPA website where you can find out if your land is designated as a wetland. The Sacketts' property did not appear there. (The EPA would later claim, by way of explanation, that "the website isn't perfect.")

The Sacketts demanded that the EPA provide details, in

writing, spelling out what they had done wrong. After they sent two certified letters to the agency, they finally received something in writing—seven months later.

What they received was an EPA-issued compliance order, which subjected the Sacketts to a fine of $75,000 a day for violating the Clean Water Act. According to the agency, the Sacketts' property was designated as a wetland, yet their neighbors have built houses on either side of their lot, and the lot already has established sewage lines. The lot does not harbor a lake, pond, or stream. The EPA's wetland claims just did not add up. With the $75,000 fines accumulating every single day, the Sacketts felt hopeless.

The compliance ordered required that the Sacketts remove the gravel they had placed on their land, put the site back the way that it was, plant supposedly wetlands-friendly plants that were not native to the site, fence the site, and maintain the property for five years. Then they were eligible to apply for a building permit. Obviously, these requirements are absurd and hypocritical, to say the least. The EPA demands that you return the site to its "natural" state, but then add plants that are not native to the site? Not to mention that the Sacketts were forced to fulfill these dictates on their own time and expense.

This family was being bullied by their own government. "You go to bed with that on your mind every night," said Mike Sackett. "It's been painful personally. It's been painful on our business." But the Sacketts continued to stand up to the bullying. Just like David, they did not let the Goliath-like agency walk all over them. They were not going to stand idly by while their rights were unjustly stripped away. So they went looking for answers.

When Chantell Sackett asked for evidence that their property was indeed a wetland, the EPA directed her to the Fish and
Wildlife National Wetlands Inventory, which clearly showed
that their lot was *not* on an existing wetland. When the EPA
refused to show proof or evidence of their claims, the Sacketts hired wetland specialists, soil scientists, and hydrologists.
These specialists *all* concluded that there were *no* wetlands of
any type on their property. So not only was the property not
registered in the official Fish and Wildlife National Wetlands
Inventory, but all of the specialists agreed that it did not harbor any wetland molecules whatsoever.

Amazingly, the power-hungry agency continued to demand
compliance. The EPA still required that the Sacketts obtain
a building permit if they wished to continue with construction. As you can imagine, getting a Clean Water Act permit
is a timely and costly process. On average, these permits cost
$270,000 and take about two years to obtain. The permit the
Sacketts required cost over ten times more than the value of
the land. It appeared as if this couple's American dream was
never going to come true—all because of invasive and tyrannical American bureaucracy.

But the Sacketts did not give up. They continued to demand
explanations. They continued to fight for their rights.

One of the most alarming problems with the EPA is the
amount of power that it allows a single bureaucrat to possess.
Compliance orders can be issued by a single EPA official on
"any evidence." This rarely constitutes a probable cause, as
seen in the Sacketts' case. Without any physical evidence of
wetlands and without any designation on the Fish and Wildlife National Wetlands Inventory, it was simply the EPA's word
against theirs—the government verses the governed.

It is often said that you can't fight city hall—but what if you can't stop city hall from constantly fighting you? The Sacketts literally had no choice.

They requested a hearing before the EPA where they could challenge the agency's claim that their property was a wetland. The EPA refused. According to the agency, the Clean Water Act does not give property owners any right to a hearing regarding compliance orders. Compliance orders are more or less just threatening letters, not enforcement actions. So the Sacketts would be forced to wait for the EPA to file an enforcement action. Throughout this waiting process, the daily $75,000 fine continued to accumulate. Seventy-five thousand dollars a day! It appeared as if the Sacketts were permanently stuck in bureaucratically controlled limbo. By the time their case was heard by the Supreme Court, their fine would total in the millions.

However, they filed their own lawsuit in federal court, arguing that the Administrative Procedure Act entitled them to a hearing before a judge. They also argued that the Clean Water Act's compliance order violated their constitutional right to due process of law. Yet the Sixth and Fourth Circuits rejected any possibility of judicial review. The courts attempted to justify the EPA's actions by stating that "Congress intended to allow the EPA to act to address environmental problems quickly and without becoming immediately entangled in litigation." Is this not a complete violation of the separation-of-powers principle? Does the EPA report to no one? Is it the be-all, end-all of regulatory action? These circuit courts essentially handed the EPA free rein over innocent Americans and their private property. The complete absurdity of this is hard even to grasp. Our government was literally telling the Sacketts that in the United States of America, you are free—unless the EPA decides to get involved, at which time your right to due process and private property becomes null and void.

The EPA claims that its ability to protect the environment would be "substantially undermined if compliance order recipients could immediately halt the agency in court," and that compliance orders "obviate the need for judicial intervention by inducing compliance." So in other words, your constitutional right to due process does not exist in the eyes of the EPA.

The government cannot take your liberty or property without first giving you due process of law. This is not my humble opinion. This is the law of the land, known as the U.S. Constitution. The EPA violates people's constitutional rights every day—and what do they say justifies it? The agency says that it does not have to go to court and it should never have to do so to defend its actions, no matter how much they infringe on the rights of American citizens. To which I shake my head and think, "What has this government come to?"

As I mentioned earlier, the EPA gives individual agents far too much power over American citizens. The Clean Water Act and other environmental statutes allow individual bureaucrats to issue orders without probable cause. Instead, their claims are supported by "any information," such as staff reports, newspaper clippings, anonymous phone tips, or pretty much anything else you can imagine. Timothy Sandefur of the Pacific Legal Foundation describes this anomaly: "What the EPA calls flexibility to compel behavior without 'defensive litigation' is, in reality, a daunting power over ordinary citizens. The agency issues over 1,000 compliance orders each year, without hearings or public proceeding, and property owners are not given notice or an opportunity to be heard."

Rather than applying a more skeptical eye to autonomous entities such as the EPA, courts generally take a deferential attitude, allowing the agencies to act as they please, except in the most extreme cases. The tragedy is that a large part of this book is dedicated to cases most Americans would no doubt consider extreme—and yet our government saw fit to let the abuse continue.

This lack of oversight and accountability is dangerous. In the words of one former Army Corps of Engineers official, "For regulatory purposes, a wetland is whatever we decide it is."

Obviously, this is a problem, and it has become an even bigger problem since the definition of wetlands used by government regulators has changed nearly ten times in thirty years. It is both a moving and amorphous target.

Courts have taken the deferential attitude to another extreme, indicating that they cannot question the "science" of what is or is not a wetland, only allowing themselves to take up whether or not the EPA has followed their own moving-target rules.

But there is some hope on the judicial front, and there is promise that checks and balances might finally be imposed on the EPA.

After the Sacketts fought for years, the Supreme Court agreed to hear their case. The Sacketts were represented by Attorney David Schiff of the Pacific Legal Foundation, which has argued that "administrative convenience should not be an excuse for dispensing with basic principles of the rule of law and striking citizens of their constitutional rights."

Court hearings began in January 2012, and the Supreme

Court justices did not seem to possess the same mindset as the circuit court judges. Schiff described the first few days of litigation by saying, "I was certainly pleased. During several points during the EPA attorney's presentation, he was interrupted by very searching and suspicious questions from the justices."

Justice Samuel Alito was most skeptical while questioning Malcolm Stewart, the Justice Department's deputy solicitor general and legal counsel for the EPA, exclaiming, "Don't you think most ordinary homeowners would say this kind of thing can't happen in the United States? You buy property to build a house. You think maybe there is a little drainage problem in part of your lot, so you start to build the house and then you get an order from the EPA which says: You have filled in wetlands, so you can't build your house; remove the fill, put in all kinds of plants; and now you have to let us on your premises whenever we want to."

And Alito was not the only justice to raise an eyebrow over the case. Justice Stephen Breyer implied that the EPA was thumbing its nose at seventy-five years of judicial precedent, during which "the courts have interpreted statutes with an eye towards permitting judicial review, not the opposite."

Mike Sackett was pleased with the initial hearings and said that he had not expected the members of the Supreme Court to skeptically question the EPA the way they did. "It was quite obvious that they were not happy with the EPA or how we've been treated," he said. "Eight out of the nine justices were asking questions [of the EPA attorney]. It was amazing, especially since we're the ones who have been going through this nightmare with the EPA for almost five years."

It was with great pleasure that we saw the Supreme Court

rule 9–0 in favor of the Sacketts in this case. Every member of the bench saw what was wrong with the EPA and our federal government giving no recourse to its citizens. But will every family that has been treated like the Sacketts have to take their case all the way to the Supreme Court to find justice?

Many problems remain. The courts rule very narrowly, simply allowing an appeal earlier in the regulatory process to give some temporary relief. The unjust rules that the EPA used to go after the Sacketts and other citizens are largely still in place. The same agency guidance methods are still being used. Similar new rules are still being written.

But the Supreme Court was unusually blunt in its opinion. The justices stated clearly and definitively that Congress must do its job and fix this mess. Until Congress explicitly defines what navigable waterways are, government abuse of this process and harassment of citizens will continue. Some states—including Idaho, in fact, where the Sacketts live—have defined "navigable waters" with commonsense definitions like whether or not you can float a log in the water, while the federal government's definition remains at best murky.

The Sackett case moved me, emotionally and intellectually. I knew there were problems regarding the EPA before, but meeting these folks and hearing their full story pushed me to write the bill that will hopefully stop such unconscionable government abuse.

Before I ran for office, when I would hear of government abuse like this, I would fume and perhaps throw something at my TV. Now I can actually do something about it. I plan to use the platform I have as a U.S. senator, for however long I have it, to fight for people like the Sacketts. They deserve better. All Americans do.

The Sacketts won their case but are still fighting for the rights of others who've been treated in the same unforgivable manner by their government. It is reassuring to know that our judicial system still has some interest in actual justice—even when Congress threatens devastating penalties for these ambiguously worded violations, leaving the detailed discretion to administrative agents. There is a reason why our Founding Fathers instituted the concept of checks and balances, and when they are not used, tyranny always emerges.

I would like to believe it impossible that any member of Congress could have imagined that the Clean Water Act would apply to a case like the Sacketts'. The act is supposed to deal with "navigable waters"; however, this case deals with "wetlands," or the lack thereof. The Clean Water Act is emblematic of, as Sandefur describes it, "the constitutional sloppiness of modern administrative agencies." This characteristic sloppiness is something all Americans should be weary of as bureaucrats run amok and bully American citizens with abandon.

The Sacketts did not deserve what their government did to them. No American does.

4

★ ★ ★

Living Every Day in Fear of Your Government

"When governments fear the people, there is liberty. When the people fear the government, there is tyranny."

—Thomas Jefferson

★ ★ ★

Robbie Wrigley is a nurse and a mother who lies awake each night in fear of her government.

Why does Mrs. Wrigley fear her own government? Because she was sentenced to eighty-seven months in prison for the "crime" of placing fill or dirt on a low-lying area of her father's land. After serving twenty-six months in a federal prison, she is now free—but still lives in constant fear that the EPA might revoke her probation and send her back to prison.

Her father, age seventy, and her father's engineer, age eighty, are still in prison. Robbie fears that if she speaks out against this injustice—even if she speaks to a congressional hearing—the government will toughen its stance and insist that her father and his engineer serve their entire prison sentences.

How did this happen in America?

Robbie Wrigley doesn't live in some third-world dictatorship. She doesn't live in Communist China. So why, in the United States of America—supposedly the best example of freedom and liberty in the world—is she both persecuted by law enforcement and living in fear of retaliation should she dare to speak out?

This wasn't always so.

In their community, the Wrigley family were known as a

hardworking and well-respected Mississippi family. They went to church, gave to charity, and were involved in many of the local civic and school associations. This was the quintessential all-American family. The Wrigleys did everything right.

They worked hard and played by the rules. We hear such praiseworthy phrases often, especially from politicians. Americans are told time and again that if they work hard and play by the rules they can be free and prosperous. The Wrigleys can tell you that this isn't always true. In fact, they were punished precisely because they did all the right things and dared to pursue the American dream.

Like millions of Americans, the Wrigleys were honest small business owners who worked to improve their community, but being upstanding, hardworking pillars of one's community apparently does not mean you are safe from the wrath of the federal government. Robbie Wrigley and her father, Robert Lucas, were wrongfully prosecuted in precisely the tyrannical manner the Founding Fathers once feared our federal government could become capable of.

John Adams, Thomas Jefferson, and Benjamin Franklin all feared an out-of-control, out-of-touch, and unaccountable federal bureaucracy that might one day acquire the power to wreak havoc upon ordinary citizens. Based on unfortunate breaches of power, as seen in Robbie Wrigley's case, the fears of our Founders have proven to be remarkably on target. They foresaw such tyranny and abuse. The men who fought to create this country would no doubt be outraged and ashamed of today's overbearing and overregulating federal government.

So what great crime did Robbie Wrigley and her father commit to attract the attention of the federal government?

Robbie Lucas Wrigley grew up in a household that was sustained by land development. Her father, Robert Lucas, began developing land in high school, continued doing so to finance his college education, and it became his livelihood.

Over the past fifty-two years, Lucas has developed over two thousand lots and has maintained a spotless reputation his entire career. He made his success by subdividing timberland north of Pascagoula, Mississippi, into two- and four-acre home sites. These sites were complete with roads, electricity, water wells, and septic tanks. Lucas was known throughout his community for personally financing the lots he sold, and he even carried the loans for people who otherwise would not have been able to buy a lot. Most of the houses on his lots were of modest design, low-income homes and trailers. Think of George Bailey in *It's a Wonderful Life*, only when the government got involved things didn't turn out so wonderful for Mr. Lucas.

Not one lot owner ever sued Lucas. He had never even had so much as a brush with the law, and was established as a well-respected and valued member of his community. Lucas's daughter, Robbie Wrigley, also lived up to her family's reputation, a schoolteacher, nurse, and mother. In her spare time, Wrigley would help her father in selling his developed land to lower-income families who were looking for affordable housing. She was on the board of the local tennis association and founded her school's booster club. Mrs. Wrigley was the classic soccer mom, who had never even gotten a speeding ticket.

So how did these normal, everyday, and exemplary Americans end up locked away in federal prison?

It began with the development of a 2,600-acre subdivision in Vancleave, Mississippi, known as Big Hill Acres. This development is twelve miles north of the Gulf coast in Jackson County, and the nearest navigable creek is over two miles away. The property is a hundred feet above sea level and covered with pine trees. The development housed over six hundred low-income families and provided them with electricity, roads, water wells, and septic tanks.

M. E. Thompson was the engineer responsible for designing the development's septic systems. He acquired the appropriate permits and went through all the appropriate measures. Mr. Thompson was an experienced engineer and all of his septic tanks followed Mississippi Health Department guidelines.

Yet these state-approved septic tanks are the reason why the Lucas family's world was turned upside down. A state functionary who oversaw the issuing of septic permits seemed to subjectively revoke one hundred of Lucas's permits, and he suddenly found himself fighting tooth and nail to have them reinstated. He was successful in the reinstatement—but this was just the beginning of a long uphill battle.

You see, in typical arrogant bureaucratic fashion, the health department functionary was not happy that her revocations had been overruled. So what did she do?—run to the federal government so she could use them as enforcers for her personal agenda. I, as an elected official, as a U.S. senator, don't have this kind of power. Why do we allow it to unelected bureaucrats?

This type of behavior coming from a federal bureaucracy is bullying at its worst, which caused complete devastation for this family.

The government enforcers brought in were none other than the Mississippi Department of Environmental Quality, the U.S. Army Corps of Engineers, and the Environmental Protection Agency. The Corps informed Lucas that Big Hill "may" violate the Clean Water Act, endangering possible "wetlands."

Yet previously, when Lucas was selling timber off of the same piece of property now in question, this same Corps of Engineers approved his sales, stating in their report that "no waterways existed," "no waterways had been built," and "no action was required."

The Corps couldn't have been any more explicit. Lucas couldn't have been any more assured that he was free and clear.

However, this time the Corps suddenly claimed there was a problem. Lucas was accused of not obtaining an EPA septic permit. However, there is little evidence that this permit even exists, as no such permit has ever been required or issued anywhere within the United States. So the EPA faulted Lucas for developing on wetlands that the agency had previously said were nonexistent, and targeted him for failing to obtain a permit that didn't even exist and had never been required of anyone in the history of this country. This is insanity. This is completely outrageous. This is completely unacceptable. There had been no reported problems with the septic tanks. In fact, the septic tank failure rate at the Big Hill Acres development was significantly better than the county average.

Jesse Beasley and his family bought a cottage in Big Hill Acres after Hurricane Katrina and have lived there ever since. The Beasleys considered themselves fortunate to have obtained the property and viewed it as helpful alternative housing for a family like themselves, who were trying to recover from a devastating natural disaster. When asked about the status of his septic tank by a government official, Mr. Beasley replied, "Our septic system is working fine. We have not had any issues."

As noted earlier, the development itself was not a wetland. It was twelve miles inland from the coast, over two miles away from a running creek, and one hundred feet above sea level. By no reasonable definition—by no government definition— was this property in any way a wetland.

But the EPA does not like being questioned. This agency gets annoyed when homeowners dare stand up for their rights. These bureaucratic tentacles of the federal government had made their decree, and the EPA was determined to make an example out of Lucas and his family—even if Lucas hadn't violated a single law. This wasn't about justice, but power and government control. Lucas fought this bureaucratic army with all his might. Unfortunately, his daughter was caught in the cross fire.

Robert Lucas, Robbie Lucas Wrigley, M. E. Thompson, and two affiliated corporations, Big Hill Acres Inc., and Consolidated Investments Inc., were convicted of "conspiring" to violate the Clean Water Act. Let me be clear—these people were not convicted of actually violating the act; they were convicted of *conspiring* to violate the act. The EPA went on to convict them of mail fraud.

Instead of succumbing to the convictions of the EPA, these "conspirators" pleaded innocent and chose to fight. They refused to surrender their rights and their private property. But their taking this stance for liberty and justice only exacerbated the EPA's vendetta.

Had they plea-bargained and pled guilty, they probably would be free now. Instead, they maintained their innocence and fought the EPA in court, where the feds unleashed the full force of their prosecutorial power on them.

However, judicial precedent forbade the court from even ruling on the key issue at hand: whether or not their land was really "wetlands." To this date, no one—"expert" government officials, the agencies themselves, no one—has truly been able to define "wetlands" consistently. It is an ambiguous term that the EPA twists to fit whatever situation they deem appropriate. "Wetlands" are simply whatever the EPA says they are, a definition that can change dramatically without rhyme or reason. Even the Supreme Court criticized the existing wetlands laws as vague and impossible to comprehend.

Herein lies the most frightening aspect of this entire debacle: The law says that a wetland must have a steady flow to a navigable body of water. As noted, this property was over two miles away from the closest stream, and the Army Corps of Engineers itself had declared it wetland-free. So how did the Wrigleys' case fall under the jurisdiction of the federal government and violate the Clean Water Act?

I am convinced that the EPA intentionally set out to make an example of Robbie Wrigley and her father because they chose to make a stand, because these hardworking, decent, and upstanding American citizens would not go down on bended knee. They refused to submit. Robbie and her father were clearly singled out to prove a point. The federal government wanted not justice, but to send a clear message: Do not question us, do not defy us, do not cross us—we are the government.

From the government's perspective, a fire had been ignited, and so the agencies turned a complicated wetlands legal issue into a kangaroo court. Judge Louis Guirola, renowned for prosecuting white-collar crimes, presided over the case. The odds were against Lucas and Wrigley from the beginning of the seven-week trial. The jury was composed of twelve working-class people. These jurors were an honest representation of the American population, and they were hard pressed to understand the complex EPA regulations that even Supreme Court justices admit they can't figure out. The prosecutors demagogued their court audience, inflaming the jury by portraying Lucas and Wrigley as rich, greedy, corporate-minded individuals who had set out to exploit and hurt their working-class clients.

The EPA had a very weak legal argument—so instead they used verbal smoke and mirrors to paint a falsified image of Lucas and his family. The prosecutors portrayed Lucas as an arrogant and heartless individual who sat high upon his golden throne, while his clients lived in filth due to septic tank failures. They wanted the jurors to view Lucas as a greedy businessman who was knowingly taking advantage of poor people living in manufactured housing. Nothing could be further from the truth.

The prosecution sought out the Big Hill Acres homeowners and tried to convince them that they had been defrauded by Lucas and his daughter. These prosecutors encouraged the homeowners to join the government's side in criminally charging their developer. The government even held a town hall, trolling for anyone willing to register a complaint against the Wrigleys.

Despite their bullying, only thirty-six out of three hundred homeowners decided to legally pursue the Lucas family. Nearly 90 percent of the homeowners refused even this level of government coercion. That's because the residents of Big Hill Acres knew better. These people had a conscience—and refused to wrongfully portray Lucas and Wrigley under oath.

Lucas and Wrigley argued that there was no proof they had violated the Clean Water Act and that they had never conspired to do so. Randy Wrigley, Robbie's husband, makes a legitimate argument on his wife's behalf when he points out, "They accused her of a conspiracy. It's preposterous. They did not conspire about this, but [in a court of law] you have to prove that you didn't conspire. How do you prove that?"

After the arguments were presented, the jurors were instructed by the judge to deliberate. This type of deliberation should have taken several hours of discussion before a vote was held. There were over forty counts of wetland charges that needed to be carefully muddled through. This was obviously not a simple decision that could be made hastily. But the jury, exhausted and bored with the seven-week trial, appeared before the court with a decision after just three hours of deliberation. They found the defendants guilty on all counts.

Lucas's two corporations were sentenced to five years' probation and were subject to $1.4 million in costs for mitigating the Jackson County wetlands. The corporations also faced more than $5 million in fines. Robert Lucas was sentenced to nine years in federal prison, while Thompson, the engineer behind Big Hill Acres, and Robin Wrigley were sentenced to seven years each.

The verdict was reached just after Hurricane Katrina destroyed the Gulf coast. The Wrigleys and many of their neighbors were tragically affected by the hurricane. Many of their homes were destroyed. Yet Big Hill Acres—the government's purported "wetlands" that would bankrupt the Wrigleys and land them in jail—did not flood during or after Hurricane Katrina.

For days after the natural disaster, Robbie and her husband spent time visiting various homeowners in need and filling up generators, so that elderly and ill neighbors on respirators would not die.

Yet immediately after the cleanup, Robbie had to move out of her family's FEMA trailer and straight into a federal penitentiary. "You try to do everything you can to help your neighbors and then the government ends up prosecuting you. It makes you want to get in a shell and hide," she says.

Though educated as a teacher and nurse, Robbie Wrigley found herself working in the kitchen of Marianna federal prison, while her nineteen-month-old son grew up without a mother. What did she do to deserve this? She ran errands for her father and helped him maintain his development property. Governor Haley Barbour, Lieutenant Governor Phil Bryant, and Mississippi secretary of state Delbert Hosemann all wrote letters to President George W. Bush asking for clemency for Robbie Wrigley. President Bush did nothing.

Former U.S. attorney Dunn Lampton was disgusted by the government's acrimonious actions against Robbie Wrigley and her family and took it upon himself to contact the federal prosecutor on the case and argue for Wrigley's freedom. The prosecutor apparently had a change of heart after the trial was over. He felt that Robbie's sentence was too harsh, and by the grace of God, he found his sense of compassion and used an arcane rule to have her released. Still, Robbie served over two years in prison before she was released.

Today, this nightmare is far from over. Mrs. Wrigley still lives in fear of her own government. She worries that the EPA might revoke her probation and send her back to prison. She is afraid to utilize her freedom of speech. She has had all of her rights unmercifully stripped from her once and now fears it could happen again.

Robbie has already missed her daughter's first words and first steps. She can't vote. She can't exercise her Second Amendment rights. The abject fear in her life, every day, means she does not feel safe exercising her First Amendment rights either.

It is understandable that Robbie fears that if she speaks out—even if she speaks to a congressional hearing—the government will make her father, Robert Lucas, and his engineer, M. E. Thompson, serve their entire prison sentences (which they likely will, because most federal crimes are not eligible for parole).

Wrigley describes her daily nightmare: "It's crazy. You cannot believe the things the government can do to you. I was so in the dark about why I was being convicted. They like to take people like me and make an example of them." No American is safe from the ever-extending and always-strengthening grasp of these federal agencies.

But now Robbie Wrigley's main concern is freeing her father and M. E. Thompson, both still serving unjust sentences. These people deserve to have a voice. Their story should be shouted from every rooftop. What the Wrigleys have been forced to go through should be a national outrage.

After all, this is America, land of the free, right?

5

★ ★ ★

American Hero

"The true soldier fights not because he hates what is in front of him, but because he loves what is behind him.

—G. K. CHESTERTON

* * *

Where are our heroes today?

We speak often of those who fight for our freedom overseas, and we should. There are many sacrifices made by our men and women in the military to spread the flame of freedom around the world. Thanks to them, America has been a beacon of liberty and a grand example of freedom for people all over the world for 236 years.

Our Founding Fathers spent, and often gave, their lives to build a new country, where men could truly be free, a nation where the rights granted to us by our Creator could not be trampled on or taken by government.

Unfortunately, this is what government too often tries to do. When it does, what exactly can an ordinary citizen do to fight back? Too often the threat of a long, expensive, and exhausting battle against one's own government is enough to stop anyone in their tracks.

Not so for John Rapanos.

Seventy-seven-year-old Rapanos is a grandfather to six grandchildren and a longtime property developer in Midland, Michigan. He has spent two decades of his life fighting against the out-of-control bureaucrats in the EPA and Army Corps of Engineers.

From 1988 to 2006, John Rapanos and his wife, Judith, fought daily to keep their most basic rights. They had to fight for their freedoms in a country that has always prided itself as being "the land of the free."

The EPA was ruthless in its aggression toward the Rapanoses. The government set out to make an example of this family, but the Rapanoses did not falter or succumb to government pressure. They did not live in fear. They pressed forward bravely and relentlessly for their basic constitutional rights. This twenty-year saga began in 1989, when Rapanos began preparing a property in Midland for development. After he broke ground, the EPA intervened and ordered him to obtain a costly federal building permit before resuming construction.

Like any good developer, Rapanos had already obtained the necessary local building permits. However, he refused to obtain the irrationally expensive and unjustified federal permits dictated by the EPA—he knew he was not violating any law or even any known regulation.

The EPA agents claimed his land was a wetland. Rapanos contested this, however, pointing out that his property was twenty miles away from the closest navigable water in Saginaw Bay.

Let me reiterate that. Mr. Rapanos's property was *twenty miles* away from the closest navigable waterway. Still, the EPA thought it had regulatory oversight of the property and designated it a wetland.

As a professional developer, Mr. Rapanos knew the ridiculousness of the EPA's claim and continued building. The EPA then criminally charged him with violating the Clean Water Act. This began an exhausting twenty-year legal battle.

The case was first heard before a judge in 1993. Government attorneys sought criminal charges against Rapanos and wanted him imprisoned. However, Judge Lawrence Zatkoff condemned the government and its agenda against Rapanos, rejecting the EPA's call for an absurdly long sixty-three-month prison sentence.

Judge Zatkoff saw this sentence as too harsh, and for good reason. Earlier that same day he had overseen the trial of a local drug dealer—a true criminal—who was being sentenced to ten months' jail time. Judge Zatkoff was outraged at the ruthless and personal attack on Rapanos, calling him "the kind of person the Constitution was passed to protect."

John Rapanos, an upstanding American citizen, was facing sixty three months behind bars, $10 million in fines, and $3 million in mitigation fees. He would also lose eighty acres of his property if the court did in fact declare it a "wetland."

Judge Zatkoff summed up the injustice best when he stated, "So here we have a person who comes to the United States and commits crimes of selling dope and the government asks me to put him in prison for ten months. And then we have an American citizen who buys land, pays for it with his own money, and he moves some sand from one end to the other and the government wants me to give him sixty-three months in prison. Now, if that isn't our system gone crazy, I don't know what is. And I am not going to do it."

The EPA attorneys were determined, however. John Rapanos was their target and they were not going to let him beat them. They had set their sights on his successful prosecution, one way or another, and they were not going to give up that easily.

Luckily, neither was Rapanos.

The government attorneys successfully appealed Judge

Zatkoff's ruling. The Rapanos case was then ordered to the court of appeals, where the case would be considered based on the court's earlier decision in the *Solid Waste Agency of Northern Cooke County v. U.S. Army Corps of Engineers* (*SWANCC*) case. In that case, the Supreme Court had ruled against the government's broad authority under the Clean Water Act in 2001.

The Supreme Court had rejected the Corps' claim that it could regulate an *isolated* intrastate lake in Illinois merely because migratory birds used it. Isolated intrastate waters lacking any meaningful connection to navigable waterways, the Court held, did not constitute as "waters of the United States" and were not subject to CWA and federal regulation.

Basically, the Corps and EPA argued that if a bird could conceivably have flown from a designated wetlands area in another state and landed on your cattle pond, then somehow your cattle pond was now "connected" to the interstate wetlands. This argument makes even President Obama's stretch of the commerce clause seem almost quaint.

What is more insulting and dangerous is that for years this stretching of the imagination concocted by an unelected bureaucrat was enforced as law until the court struck it down.

Finally, using the *SWANCC* decision as a guide, the Supreme Court struck down this lunacy and ruled that Rapanos should not be convicted.

But as I noted earlier, the EPA was on a mission to ruin Rapanos. For the agency this wasn't about justice, but revenge. They were not going to give up their prosecution of this innocent American citizen. Federal prosecutors changed their argument and began claiming that they had authority over the Rapanoses' property because the land was "hydrologically connected" to navigable waters—even though the property is twenty miles away from said waters. The court again ruled in Rapanos's favor, but on appeal the Sixth Circuit harbored a narrow interpretation of *SWANCC* and reinstated his conviction.

The EPA ruthlessly danced with glee from court to court, vehemently pursuing the prosecution and conviction of John Rapanos. The agency was determined to bankrupt him and take possession of his property. His ordeal lasted four more years.

Then, on October 11, 2005, the Supreme Court announced it would finally hear the tragic story of Mr. Rapanos—a case in which federal regulators sought for two decades to throw a seventy-year-old grandfather of six in prison and demand he pay millions in fees and fines all because he failed to get a federal permit before moving sand on his property.

I wish I were making this up.

In June 2006, a divided Supreme Court, in *Rapanos v. United States*, ruled that the U.S. Army Corps of Engineers must show a "significant nexus" between a wetland and navigable water in order to assert regulatory control under the Clean Water Act.

But the ruling, which attempted to define navigable waters, was still murky. With a 4–4–1 split, it lacked a clear directive to the EPA.

What is the definition of navigable waters?

According to the Corps, the "waters of the United States" include "all waters used for intrastate commerce," "all interstate waters and wetlands," "all tributaries or impoundments of such waters," and, most significantly, "all other waters such as intrastate lakes, rivers, streams (including intermittent streams, mudflats, sandblast, wetlands, sloughs, prairie pot-holes, wet meadows, playa lakes, or natural ponds) the use, degradation, or destruction of which could affect interstate or foreign commerce."

"Wetlands adjacent to waters (other than waters that are themselves wetlands)" are also included in the Corps' defini-tion. Yet even according to that broad, ambiguous definition, Rapanos was not in violation of the Clean Water Act. Again, the closest stream was over twenty miles away. The injustice and abuse orchestrated by the EPA simply does not make sense.

During the Supreme Court battle, the EPA premised its enforcement proceeding on a "hydrological connection" between navigable water and Rapanos's property. The hydro-logical connection test, formulated by some field office of the Army Corps of Engineers, postulates that federal authority extends to any channel through which water flows into navi-gable waters—whether the channel is on the surface or in the ground, supports intermittent or steady flows, carries mole-cules or floods. Based on this outrageous test, the federal gov-ernment brought criminal charges against Rapanos because the sand he moved on his property "backfilled" intermittently saturated bits of land on his property, and because of the hypo-thetical threat that some of that sand might be carried by rain-water through old runoff drains and, after a journey through culverts, creeks, and ditches, end up in the Kawkawlin River, twenty miles away.

The prosecution's argument was far-fetched, to say the least.

The Court was split in its decision. Five justices—Scalia, Thomas, Roberts, Alito, and Kennedy—were not convinced of Rapanos's conviction and rejected the arguments presented by the prosecution. But the justices had varying opinions and interpretations of the definition of "navigable waters" and the federal jurisdiction granted through the Clean Water Act.

Justice Scalia, on behalf of four justices, determined that the Clean Water Act's definition of "navigable waters" applies to "relatively permanent, standing or flowing" waters "with a continuous surface connection" to navigable waters.

Justice Stevens also wrote an opinion on behalf of four justices, asserting that the Clean Water Act's definition of "navigable waters" applies to any parcel of land or water that drains to or is in the extended watershed of navigable waters.

Justice Kennedy defined "navigable waters" as applying to any land or water that has a "significant nexus" to navigable waters, and the plot of land or water must be significant enough "to perform important functions for an aquatic system incorporating navigable waters." Kennedy's definition did not go on to explain the process of the "significant nexus" test, thus placing more ambiguity and broad power in the hands of the government.

Although property rights supporters saw this Court ruling in a positive light, there is no question that the *Rapanos* decision left our clean water laws a little murkier than they were before. The decision had an immediate positive effect, though—in showing bureaucrats at the EPA that they do not simply get to imagine laws and then enforce them.

The state of property rights in the aftermath of *Rapanos v. United States* was not a sea change, but rather a logical sequel to *SWANCC*.

In the *Rapanos* decision, the Supreme Court reaffirmed the existence of both statutory and constitutional limits on the scope of federal regulatory jurisdiction over private lands and waters.

The Supreme Court rejected the EPA and the Army Corps' expansive interpretation of their own authority, and reiterated that federal regulatory authority only extends to those wetlands that have "significant nexus" to navigable waters of the United States.

Since this decision was handed down in 2006, our country has seen numerous court battles over the same ambiguity that *Rapanos* was supposed to clear up. Our government has yet to agree on and concretely define the term "wetlands" and "navigable waters." How can American citizens be prosecuted for something that the courts, Congress, and bureaucratic agencies cannot agree on? Furthermore, how does one know they are violating a law if the law itself is not firmly and concretely understood by all branches of government?

Our government's constitutional ignorance is something that all Americans should be wary of. Congress enacts broadly worded statutes threatening devastating penalties for vaguely worded violations—and leaves administrative officials to then muddy the law through drawn-out litigation with the discretion to fill in the details. The *Rapanos* decision was not by any means a landmark one, but it was a step in the right direction and a glimmer of hope in our bureaucratic-imposed world. Another step was taken in the more recent *Sackett* decision, which I covered in an earlier chapter.

But once again, even with "victory" from the courts, there is not enough relief and certainly not enough change in policy at the EPA.

Why?

The answer is simple. In the *Rapanos* case, Justice Scalia tried to bring a simple, real-world, easily understood definition of wetlands and navigable waterways to the issue. He was not supported by his colleagues, and his words, while clarifying, are not binding on the EPA. Scalia noted this in his decision on the *Sackett* case, where he called on Congress to fix the problem it has created and the EPA has exacerbated, by passing into law a definition of navigable waterways.

My bill, the Defense of Environment and Property Act of 2012, would do just that, including using essentially the definition first propounded by Justice Scalia in the *Rapanos* case.

With a bill that so clearly solves a huge problem, you would think I would have an easy time moving it, or at least getting support among Republicans who say they are for property rights.

Well, if you thought that, you haven't yet met the United States Senate members and the army of lobbyists on Capitol Hill united.

6

★ ★ ★

More Heroes, More Horror Stories

"Life, liberty, and property do not exist because men have made laws. On the contrary, it was the fact that life, liberty, and property existed beforehand that caused men to make laws in the first place."

—FREDERIC BASTIAT

* * *

Unfortunately the aggression by our government against business and property owners does not stop with the horror stories you've read thus far. Here are more examples of law-abiding, hardworking Americans who've been unjustly targeted by the bullying agencies of our federal government.

Ocie Mills

Ocie Mills and his son, Carey, made their American dream a reality in 1986 when they purchased two parcels of property in Santa Rosa County, Florida. This property was covered with oak trees and Spanish moss, and was adjacent to that county's East Bay in the Spanish Landing subdivision. It was the perfect place for the father and son to build their dream homes. As lifelong residents of Florida, they had always dreamed of owning a house on the water. In order to make this dream a reality, Ocie Mills obtained a building permit from Santa Rosa County and had state officials come survey his land, flagging the area near the shore that was protected by law. The Mills family went through all the necessary steps in order to build on their property—or so they thought.

One day in 1986, the Millses were unloading nineteen loads of building sand onto their property when federal agents arrived with a cease-and-desist order. According to the government, Ocie and Carey Mills were in violation of the Clean Water Act for polluting the navigable waters of the United States.

This was not the first time the federal government had intervened on Ocie Mills's property. In the 1970s, two officials from the state's Department of Environmental Regulations (DER)—now called the Department of Environmental Protection (DEP)—insisted on gaining access to Mills's land. Mills asked for federal identification, but all these officials could present were business cards. These were not enough to convince Mills of their authority, so he refused to allow them on his property without a warrant. The government officials completely disregarded his requests and continued to trespass without a warrant.

Mills recalled the scene: "The agents told me who they were and then proceeded to tell me that I couldn't clear my property because of wetland regulations. The man and I had some heated words and I told him he was trespassing and to get off my property. I was still recovering from a previous heart attack, and when things looked like they were going to get physical, I walked over to my truck and got my gun out."

Mills restrained the two officers and called the local sheriff's department. Once the police arrived, they asked the DER officials to leave the property. Three days later, the DER sued Mills for battery and reckless display of a firearm. Mills not only won the case but the presiding judge changed the precedent for the state—the state could no longer trespass on private property without a warrant. Mills was victorious, yet little did he know that this action would put him on environmental bureaucrats' hit list. Ocie Mills had become a target.

A decade later in 1989, Mr. Mills found himself in court again, fighting for his rights against the federal government. He saw this as an open-and-shut case. He never imagined that the judicial system would rule against him, so due to the rationality of his case and his lack of finances, he decided to represent himself in court. In contrast, the feds appeared in court with three attorneys from the Justice Department, the Army Corps of Engineers, and the Environmental Protection Agency.

In court, the prosecution argued that Mills's evidence was not permissible. They claimed that since federal law superseded local and state law, his building permit and state documents were irrelevant. The judge ruled in favor of the prosecution, putting Ocie and his son Carey in a federal prison for twenty-one months. Not only were they imprisoned, but they were forced to pay $5,000 in fines plus $250 in special assessments, and were required to restore their land to its "original" wetland elevation. Ocie and Carey Mills were the first to serve time in prison as "environmental criminals." Let me reiterate this: The Millses obtained every state and local permit necessary to build on their land. Yet the government in court trumped those permits and these men were forced to serve time behind bars. However, the injustice does not end there.

After serving roughly two years behind bars, Mills returned to his property and began excavating it to its "original elevation" as ordered by the federal agencies. But he refused to lower the land on his property at the request of the federal government. They were demanding he bring it down to eleven inches lower than it was when he originally purchased the lot.

Removing that much soil from the property would undoubtedly turn it into a soggy marshland or pond.

Though Mills tried to prevent his property from being ruined by government regulation, the lot no longer resembled the same plush piece of real estate he had originally invested in.

So in 1993 Mills secured an "evidentiary hearing" to solve the elevation discrepancy. This time there was a new judge behind the bench, U.S. district judge Roger Vinson. Judge Vinson described the content of the Clean Water Act as something "worthy of Alice in Wonderland." It is the source of most regulatory perils being faced by property owners. The ambiguity of the broadly worded act mandates that "a landowner who places clean fill dirt on a plot of subdivided *dry land* may be imprisoned for the statutory felony offense of discharging pollutants into the *navigable waters* of the United States." According to Vinson, the plot of land belonging to Mills "does not have the appearance of what most lay people think of as wetland."

Although Judge Vinson believed that the Millses' land was most likely not a wetland, he could not clear them of their conviction because the elevation issue had not been used as evidence, or even discussed, in the original trial.

The plot thickened in 1996 when Quentin Wise, a juror in Mills's original trial, came forward and informed officials of ethical violations performed by the jury foreman. The jury foreman from Mills's original case sought to sway the jury's view of him by disclosing information about his previous clashes with government officials. He was, of course, referring to the 1970s indiscretion with the DER. In a sworn affidavit, Wise stated:

From the beginning of the trial, Mr. Smith [the jury foreman] kept telling me about Ocie Mills' prior cases. He told me that he was familiar with Ocie Mills' prior problems and wrong doings because his son was employed with the State of Florida Water Management. During the course of the trial, Mr. Smith told me that Mills had threatened environmental people on his property with a gun and that Mills was wrong for his actions. I felt threatened and intimidated by Mr. Smith during the trial. I feel that the jury was prejudiced against the Mills' by information which we received from Mr. Smith, which was not part of the evidence shown in court.

Ocie Mills spent every dime he had with the simple intention of saving his reputation. After this drawn-out legal battle with his government, he and his family are no longer proud of their property in Santa Rosa County. It has caused them nothing but shame and stress—all due to the perils of overregulation.

Marinus Van Leuzen

Marinus Van Leuzen was a small business owner from Galveston Bay, Texas. He owned a 0.4-acre bait camp, located on a plot of land tucked between two commercially developed properties. Van Leuzen decided to build a home on his property. As he was completing construction, the Army Corps of Engineers intervened, telling him he needed to have the appropriate permits to continue building. Why? You guessed it—his property, too, had been designated a "wetland."

The Corps informed Van Leuzen that he needed to obtain six different permits in order to finish building his home. Van Leuzen found this permit process ridiculous and continued to build anyway.

Like John Pozsgai, Van Leuzen emigrated to America in order to escape a harsh dictatorship, escaping from Holland just before the Nazi invasion during World War II. He fought alongside U.S. forces in the war. His neighbors described Van Leuzen as a "hard-headed Dutchman." So it came as no surprise to anyone when he ignored the orders of the government and finished building his home without first obtaining the supernumerary permits.

As his house was nearing completion, four members of the Corps posted themselves across the street from Van Leuzen's property and recorded the last stages of construction. With the video footage as evidence, the Corps ordered a public apology from him. And "public" might be an understatement when describing the apology the government forced out of Van Leuzen.

The Corps ordered Van Leuzen to create and publically display a ten-by-twenty-foot billboard carrying a message of apology to his government. Aside from attempting to publicly shame him, the Corps fined Mr. Van Leuzen $350 per month for twelve years, required him to dig a two-foot-deep moat around his home, and ordered him to restore his land to its "original wetland" state. Yet since this land was never truly a wetland, Van Leuzen was forced to "restore" his land and "re-create" a wetland that had never really existed. This process made for an incredible expenditure that he could not afford. Then, after the "restored wetland" had been intact for eight years, Van Leuzen was forced to evacuate his house.

The government forced this liberty-seeking, freedom-fighting immigrant to pay an obscene amount of money and restore property into an unnatural and costly state; it evicted him from his home, stole his property, and then publicly shamed him for disobeying the government. The power-hungry Corps mirrors the dictatorship that Van Leuzen sought to escape by emigrating to America. The irony of his ordeal should put a bad taste in the mouth of anyone who has read the U.S. Constitution.

Bill Ellen

Bill Ellen is a well-respected environmental engineer who works in the coastal region of Maryland. In 1987, he was hired to construct duck ponds on thirty-two hundred acres on the Paul Tudor Jones II estate, on Maryland's Eastern Shore. Ellen jumped through many hoops to obtain the proper permits to build these ponds, in all obtaining thirty-eight different permits, as well as assurance from the Army Corps of Engineers regarding one action that would've affected the wetlands of Maryland. The Corps gave him their approval and he began construction.

The first discrepancies arose in 1989, when the Corps changed its definition of "wetlands." The new definition established that "acreage in the county from 84,000 acres to 259,000 acres will be classified as a wetland." Thus the Corps ordered Ellen to cease construction. But he was not even violating this new definition—plus he had preapproved consent from the Army Corps. Ellen had a representative from the Soil Conservation Service of the Department of Agriculture inspect his construction site. The SCS representative cleared him, saying that he was not harming any wetlands.

If only this were the end. Several days passed and a member of the Army Corps appeared with the SCS official to order him to stop construction immediately, insisting that Ellen was filling wetlands. If this is not a prime example of government intimidation, I don't know what is.

An outraged Ellen argued that the government's own expert from the SCS had given him the green light just days prior. He informed them that contractors had already begun the building process. Permits were obtained and he had been given the go-ahead by various government agencies several times before he broke ground on construction. To stop at that point would've resulted in costly penalties to the construction companies and property owners.

The government workers threatened to tie Ellen up for decades with expensive litigation, so alas, he finally ceased construction. After the cease-and-desist order was received and abided by, Ellen had workers move two truckloads of dirt from one end of the property to the other, as a means of cleaning up the work site. So the Army Corps of Engineers indicted him, charging him with contaminating a wetland by moving the dirt and thus violating the cease-and-desist order he was given in 1989.

The well-respected environmental engineer from Maryland was convicted and served six months in prison, while his employer and owner of the property, Paul Tudor Jones II, avoided trial by paying $1 million in fines and donating $1 million to the National Fish and Wildlife Foundation. So you can have your rights, if and only if you can afford to pay the government for them. Coincidentally, to this date, the

Corps employee who initially cleared Ellen's construction plan cannot be found for comment.

The Seashell House

This story, although not directly related to wetland issues, also portrays the outrageous lengths landowners often have to go to in order to simply build on their property. Sometimes these require interactions so baffling that they are almost humorous, as author James V. DeLong explains in his book *Property Matters*. This was the case for one landowner in Pacific Grove, California, who wished to build a home on a 1.1-acre lot on the Monterey Peninsula. In order to have his building plans approved, he was required to attend twenty-plus public hearings and obtain the approval of the architectural review board, the planning commission, the city council, and the California Coastal Commission. According to the records, this process took over three years and cost over $600,000.

During one of the dozens of hearings held regarding this property, an architectural review board member said, "In my former life as a seagull, I was flying up and down the California coastline and saw your house built shaped as a seashell." And because his house plan did not match the seashell-shaped house this board member *envisioned in her previous life as a bird*, she voted against approving any of his plans.

Some would argue this board member to be certifiably insane. Others would say the insanity charge isn't even arguable. But since this person who holds a position of government authority believes to have seen and enjoyed the view of a seashell-shaped home on the property in question, the landowner did not receive approval. This landowner's American dream and basic constitutional right to private property was stifled due to a person in a position of power who is delusional at best. This is literally crazy—and if this story does not illustrate the perils of power-hungry government interventionists, then I do not know what does.

Kelo v. City of New London

In 2002, Steven Greenhut of thefreemanonline.org published a story describing the culture shock his sister-in-law had experienced while visiting Poland. Upon returning home, she furiously explained the injustice practiced by the former communist country. According to the story, a friend of hers owned a lavish country home in the Polish countryside. The home was so lovely that it caught the eye of a Polish government official, who entangled the homeowner in litigation so he could seize the property for himself. The government official wanted the home, so with the help of the court system, he simply took it.

We would like to pretend that nothing like this ever happens in America, land of the free. But in reality, situations like this have occurred and will keep occurring thanks to the Supreme Court decision *Kelo v. City of New London.*

Susette Kelo owned a house in New London, Connecticut. She had purchased the home in 1997 and through a labor of love completely restored it, making it truly her own. Kelo's pink house was located in a family-friendly neighborhood that was the quintessence of an ideal American community.

A year later in 1998, the pharmaceutical giant Pfizer began

construction on a new plant in New London. The corporate giant convinced the city that it deserved the land in Kelo's neighborhood more than she and her neighbors did. The city utilized its power of eminent domain, which enables the local government to take private property and designate it for public use. Though Kelo was compensated, the government seized her property in the name of "local economic development." Thus the City of New London provided the New London Development Corporation with a blank check and free rein over these private homes. Kelo and her neighbors received a notice of condemnation from the NLDC in November 2000.

The members of the community fought for their rights and took their case all the way to the Supreme Court. In a horrific turn of events for private property owners across the United States, the courts ruled in the favor of the City of New London and the NLDC, thus giving local governments the right to seize private property under eminent domain in the name of the broadly defined term "economic development." This was a dangerous landmark decision in U.S. law.

In his dissenting opinion, Justice Clarence Thomas wrote:

Today's decision is simply the latest in a string of our cases construing the Public Use Clause to be a virtual nullity, without the slightest nod to its original meaning. In my view, the Public Use Clause, originally understood, is a meaningful limit on the government's eminent domain power. Our cases have strayed from the Clause's original meaning, and I would reconsider them....So-called "urban renewal" programs provide some compensation for the properties they take, but no compensation is possible for the subjective value of these lands to the individuals displaced and the indignity inflicted by uprooting them from their homes.

Justice Sandra Day O'Connor also expressed outrage in her dissent on *Kelo v. City of New London*:

[The] fallout from this decision will not be random. The beneficiaries are likely to be those citizens with disproportionate influence and power in the political process, including large corporations and development firms. As for the victims, the government now has license to transfer property from those with fewer resources to those with more. The Founders cannot have intended this perverse result.

On the seventh anniversary of the *Kelo* decision in June 2012, I cosponsored a bill with Senator John Cornyn that would strengthen private property rights and limit the government's power of eminent domain, the Protection of Homes, Small Businesses, and Private Property Act of 2012. Our bill sought the "protection of homes, small businesses and other private property rights against government seizures and other unreasonable government interference is a fundamental principal and core commitment of our nation's founders."

In the end, Pfizer wished to build a hotel and offices that were meant to improve their corporate facilities. While Kelo and her neighbors lost their homes, the local and state governments spent $78 million to bulldoze the private neighborhood to clear space for "desirable" and economically stimulating facilities. To this day, the neighborhood sits vacant—no hotel or office facility was ever built.

All of this happened not in China, or North Korea, or the old Soviet Union. This happened in the United States of America.

These personal testimonies and stories of government abuse illustrate the uphill battle all Americans face when it comes to protecting our constitutional rights. Our private property rights are under attack. Mills, Ellen, and Van Leuzen have all been fined, publicly shamed, or even imprisoned for "wetlands" violations. But these three Americans have even more in common than just their petty violations against a dense and ambiguously regulated law—these three Americans all stood up for themselves. They put their foot down. They did not succumb to the abuses of power and they did not simply pay a fine and walk away with their tails between their legs. Mills, Ellen, and Van Leuzen all fought for their basic constitutional rights, only to be prosecuted in an even harsher manner for doing so. These citizens were specifically targeted for standing up for their rights as opposed to turning the other cheek to government overregulation and power-hungry bureaucrats.

This is not the United States of most Americans' perception and loyalty, and yet it is the United States. Our Founding Fathers must be rolling over in their graves at the injustice our government perpetrates against its own citizens every day.

7

★ ★ ★

How Can We Solve the Problem?

"The men who administer public affairs must first of all see that everyone holds on to what is his, and that private men are never deprived of their goods by public men."

—CICERO

* * *

My blood boils when I think of what our government is doing to our own people.

When I began my campaign for the U.S. Senate one of the first people I met was Matth Toebben of northern Kentucky. Matth came to America as a teenager from Germany, with nothing but the desire to work and belief in the American dream. His success and his desire for the next generation to find the same success is precisely what we should all be extolling—not the divisive politics of envy being practiced by the president and many in the Democratic Party.

Matth told me countless stories of the government placing obstacles in his way, but one in particular captured my attention. Matth told me about a busybody neighbor of his who reported him to the EPA. What was Matth doing wrong, exactly? He was riding around on his bulldozer. He was trying to conserve the integrity of a cattle pond that was being lost to erosion.

A praiseworthy effort, right? Not if you're the EPA.

The EPA decided to visit Matth with a phalanx of lawyers, demanding that he cease and desist improving his pond. These government agents wanted his pond returned to its previous state. They threatened to fine him $25,000 a day.

Now, Matth had not become a success by being a shrinking violet. These agents no doubt intended to charge him with something, but they really didn't realize who they were messing with. Although he could afford many attorneys and even employs in-house counsel, he arrived at the meeting on his land, alone, armed with only one thing: the original legislation.

He pulled it out of his pocket and asked them, in his German-American accent, "Have you read the bill?" The government bullies simply scoffed and looked away. He repeated, "Have you read the bill?" No one answered. Complete silence. So Matth proceeded to read them the pertinent passage: "farms are exempt." He then added, "And you can get the hell off my land!" Mr. Toebben later went on to help make changes in the state law to protect landowners from this kind of harassment.

The case of Jim Starr illustrates how Big Brother not only obstructs progress but also saps the spirit of entrepreneurs. As Peyton Knight writes for the property rights advocacy group the Property Rights Foundation of America:

Jim Starr purchased eleven acres of beautiful agricultural property on the Long Beach peninsula, located in Pacific County, Washington. It was here where he would settle with his family and pursue his passion of farming. The conditions on the peninsula were perfect for cultivating certain types of mushrooms. Full of entrepreneurial spirit, Jim planned to grow and harvest a diverse variety of mushrooms for sale in multiple markets. He spent $100,000 of his own money to renovate an old barn, thereby creating an office, laboratory and shop. Jim would have gourmet mushrooms for restaurants and mushrooms that produce the anti-carcinogenic Taxol for the medical industry. He would even produce mushrooms that contain a certain proprietary enzyme, that when added to straw, becomes an essential tool in cleaning up oil spills. Everything was set. He had jumped through the necessary hoops, purchased a work permit and filed a Pacific County Development Application. Jim was ready to begin his venture. That was five years ago. It is 2003 and Jim has yet to harvest a single mushroom or groom a single spore, and likely never will.

Instead, Jim has been mired in a five-year battle with the Army District Corps of Army Engineers of Seattle, Washington—fighting for the right to farm on his officially designated "agricultural" property. The Corps claims that Jim's property, although historically used for farming and even classified for tax purposes as "agricultural," is in fact a wetland, and therefore off-limits to any sort of external disruption. But this is no ordinary wetland. This wetland is the result of the local government's neglect and mismanagement.

The peninsula where Jim lives contains a series of drainage ditches, which when properly maintained, are essential to flood control on the low-lying peninsula. The ditches were originally constructed 80 years ago by the Civilian Conservation Corps to collect excess rainwater and carry it safely out to the surrounding ocean and bay. The Pacific County government now owns the easement for these ditches, and residents of Long Beach peninsula (including Jim) pay a "flood control" tax, ostensibly for maintenance of these channels. However, Pacific County neglects to care for the ditches, leaving them clogged and virtually inoperable. The result of this neglect is overly saturated farmland—which of course the Army Corps of Engineers considers a wetland.

The Corps came out to inspect Jim's operation and told him that a thorough environmental impact study would have to be conducted on his land. The study, of course, would be funded out of Jim's pocket to the tune of a few thousand dollars. Reluctantly, Jim agreed to the arrangement.

He was subjected to repeated bullying by the Corps and the county government, Jim said, including a threatening letter from the Assistant Director of the Pacific County Department of Community Development, who told Jim: "You will need to immediately cease all work in the wetlands and apply for review and permits. Failure to do so within the next 15 days will result in formal enforcement action against you and the contractor." Having already sought numerous permits and reviews only to be ignored by the District Corps of Army Engineers, Jim slowly began to give up the fight to farm mushrooms. When the Corps finally did take action on Jim's case, they told him that his farm would violate the rules governing wetlands because of the gravel foundation required for mushroom beds.

Jim was dejected but not content to merely live out his life on a large piece of property that the government was trying to render useless. Moreover, even though Jim's land is officially designated as agricultural property, Jim must pay a "best use" property tax until he can show an income from crops produced on his land. This means that the failure to utilize his land for growing crops for profit would result in roughly a 60% increase in his property tax burden.

Ever resourceful, Jim decided that he would build a vineyard on his farmland instead. Finally, reaching the height of his frustration, Jim decided to forge ahead. He began to preliminarily work the property in preparation for his vineyard.

Shortly thereafter, the county and the Corps returned to Jim and demanded that he once again cease and desist or face further action. They explained to Jim, this time with more than a hint of finality, that his property was a valuable wetland, and therefore, is barred from agricultural use

Jim Starr said that he did not know what else he could do. He has given up trying to farm his land.

In his obituary, Marinus Van Leuzen is described as "not solely a World War II hero. He was also a hero of the 1990's. He was one of the rare victims of the environmental police who did everything in his capacity to let the country know about the injustices imposed on him and to seek retribution in the courts for the violation of his civil rights."

Author Carol W. LaGrasse describes Van Leuzen's story in "How Environmentalism Is Being Used as a Tool to Instill Terror into American Citizens" (published by the Property Rights Foundation of America): "After his modest, attractive house is in place on a lot where a decrepit bait camp was situated, his septic system installed, with all local building permits, on land the U.S. Army Corps of Engineers designated 'uplands' on a prominent highway in a developed area," the

EPA "discovered that Marinus Van Leuzen violated the law," then cited him for a "wetlands" violation. After being forced to pay an obscene fine and do ridiculous things to his property by government decree, came the coup de grâce: Van Leuzen was ordered to erect a giant ten-by-twenty-foot billboard of apology on State Highway 37. For eight long years, the federal government harassed an eighty-eight-year-old World War II veteran who fought for his adopted country and forced him to to apologize, when he'd done nothing wrong.

Reining in Government Bullies

Instead of just fuming against our out-of-control federal bureaucracy, I vowed to do something to end the harassment of ordinary Americans. The bullying of job creators and property owners must end.

So many of the existing EPA rules are bad, and they are getting worse. Some in Congress have stressed to me that we should either let the problem be solved by the courts, in cases like *Rapanos* and *Sackett*, or fight the EPA rule by rule, guidance by guidance.

There are many problems with this approach, not the least of which is that "wetlands," "navigable waters," and other such phrases and definitions will serve as the basis for rulings, legal discussions, and further regulations. These are definitions that should have been made by Congress years ago, not by unaccountable government agencies.

What is a "navigable stream," exactly? Well, as one Corps agent admitted, "whatever we say it is." The Supreme Court didn't define navigable waters, but it did say, at least, that citizens have the right to contest in court the Corps' assertions concerning what constitutes a wetland.

It remains a dangerous situation, though, because the definition of "navigable" is still nebulous and arbitrarily decided by the Corps. Congress has abdicated its responsibility to provide clear laws and guidelines for regulators and citizens to follow.

And if the problem exists because of Congress, only Congress can truly solve it.

The courts can give small victories to property rights activists who are willing to stand up and fight. This happened in March 2012 when the Supreme Court ruled that the Sacketts had the right to challenge the EPA's compliance order in court.

But in a concurring opinion, Justice Samuel Alito noted that to truly fix this problem, Congress must "do what it should have done in the first place: provide a reasonably clear rule regarding the reach of the Clean Water Act.... Allowing aggrieved property owners to sue under the Administrative Procedures Act is better than nothing, but only clarification of the reach of the Clean Water Act can rectify the underlying problem."

I could not agree more with Justice Alito.

That's why I have introduced the Defense of Environment and Property Act of 2012, in order to do precisely what Justice Alito asked—bring common sense back to federal water policy.

The bill will do the following:

- It will redefine "navigable waters" to explicitly clarify that waters must actually be navigable, or "permanent, standing, or continuously flowing bodies of water that form geographical features commonly known as streams, oceans, rivers and lakes that are connected to waters that are navigable-in-fact."

- Ephemeral or intermittent streams—the streams that sometimes form when rain falls—will be excluded from federal jurisdiction
- The EPA and the Army Corps will be stopped from regulating or "interpreting" the definition of navigable waters without congressional authorization.
- States will once again have primary authority over the land and water within their borders.
- My bill will stop federal agents from entering private property without the express consent of the landowner.
- In order to give pause to agencies and bureaucrats, I will also force the government to pay double the value of the land to any landowner whose property value is diminished by a wetlands designation.

This bill is simple and clear, while still broad and far-reaching. It is a commonsense approach that has garnered support across the country from property rights advocates, farmers, miners, liberty activists, developers—you name it. The American people have had enough and want action.

I believe that environmental protection must not unnecessarily trample on the fundamental American right to private property. The Defense of Environment and Property Act of 2012 will restore common sense to federal jurisdiction over navigable waters and place reasonable limitations on agencies that have become dangerously out of control.

My thanks to the many activists and groups who are lending their support to the Defense of Environment and Property Act. The Pacific Legal Foundation, which represented the Sacketts, writes approvingly of it:

> Given the Corps and EPA's inability or unwillingness to acknowledge any limits to their authority over non-navigable waters, a bill of this type was perhaps inevitable. Even if Senator Paul's bill is not the last word on the subject, it will certainly enliven the debate over the scope of federal authority and perhaps result in clearer regulatory standards that would benefit both the regulating agencies and the regulated public.

FreedomWorks, one of the nation's largest Tea Party groups, has announced their support:

> Landowners should be free to do as they please with their own property. Americans have a fundamental right to private property...support S.2122, today.

The free market political advocacy group Americans for Prosperity also expressed their support:

> Regulations that help keep America's waterways clean and safe are indeed important, but these days the EPA and the Army Corps are abusing the authority they were given for a power grab at the expense of private property owners. Your legislation would rein in these out-of-control agencies and restore balance between the important goals of controlling water pollution and protecting private property rights.

The American Land Rights Association, a long-standing nationwide defender of property rights, joined the fight and promised to "do our best to encourage our members and allies to support S.2122 and ultimately help it pass Congress. [S.2122] is a necessary step toward protecting private property rights from overkill by the EPA and Army Corps of Engineers."

The Kentucky Farm Bureau, the largest general farm organization in our commonwealth, representing over half a million member families, wrote that it "compliments you for introducing S.2122. Your legislation reflects our concern about the economic well-being of not only Kentucky's farmers, but also many small business owners who are affected by excessive regulatory oversight."

James Delong, author of *Property Matters: How Property Rights Are Under Assault—And Why You Should Care*, added his support:

> Congress enacted the laws protecting the nation's waters to promote navigation and prevent pollution. Aggressive federal agencies and their environmental extremist clients have, instead, hijacked them, converting them into tools to prevent reasonable land uses and extort money from property owners for the benefit of favored environmental groups and causes. The Defense of Environment and Property Act of 2012 (S.2122) is a step toward returning federal water laws to their original purposes, and toward restoring fairness and predictability to environmental protection.

The Beseechers and the Old Guard

There are two things I have found most disturbing during my time in Washington. The first is the omnipresent groups of lobbyists and special interests who every day descend upon every Capitol Hill office in droves.

I have come to refer to them as the Beseechers. Their hands are always out. They are here to tell me why their cause/product/disease/group is by far the most—in fact possibly the *only*—one deserving of large amounts of federal dollars, tax breaks, subsidies, or special rules and privileges.

I will admit, with some pride, that unlike many of my colleagues, my day is not filled with these types of meetings. That's because word tends to spread quickly among this rather incestuous Capitol Hill community that while my door is always open to taxpayers, my office demands that anyone wanting money—for any cause no matter how necessary or noble—must first explain where the money will come from. What existing program will they delete to pay for their desired program?

If you've come for more federal money, well, guess what—we're broke.

If you've come for a special-interest tax break, you'll get yours when everyone does—no special favors.

If you've come to have a rule written to stifle your competition—you'll more likely find my office hard at work repealing rules, not creating them.

You get the idea. And often, so have the Beseechers.

But I have been very clear, if you are a person, company, industry—*anyone at all* who is looking to get the government out of your way—by all means, please step into my office, I'm all ears.

If you are among those trying to repeal bureaucracy and slash through red tape—I am the one who will help you.

If you are trying to fight back against government abuse and tyranny—I am fighting for you and with you every day.

Often the interests of liberty-loving individuals and the interests of job-creating industries will intersect. One such place (or so I thought) was in fighting the out-of-control EPA.

You see, for every Sackett family trying to build a small project, there is also a mall or shopping center developer who is so harassed to death by the government that they give up on their project.

For every John Pozsgai who wants to build on one small plot of land, there is a farming conglomerate or coal mining company that wants to use hundreds or thousands of acres.

The small businessman who wants to earn a living and create jobs is stifled, but so are larger companies interested in profits and that can create even more jobs.

Helping them all should have been easy. And as you can see from those who support the bill, those who are on the ground creating jobs in these industries did in fact support our efforts. There were many major businesses and business leaders who supported my efforts. But not all of them.

So who did not?

The Beseechers. That special, entitled class of Washington swamp dwellers who are supposed to be in the nation's capital to represent interests like farmers and coal miners, but whose main interest seems to be fat paychecks, the status quo, and currying favor with elected officials in senior positions that affect their industries.

As my staff and I worked on the Defense of Environment and Property Act, I continually heard two very different stories.

Back home in Kentucky, when talking to property owners, farmers, coal miners, and operators, I heard great support, even great joy, when I told them about the bill. The EPA, the Corps, and the various wetlands regulations were considered a complete nightmare for many constituents I spoke to. Indeed, it seemed half of the business owners in my state had a story to tell on this particular method of bullying by Washington bureaucrats.

But when I would ask my staff about the national farming, mining, or developers' groups—each representing thousands of business owners who shared this outrage at the EPA—I was told they were not helpful or supportive of the little guys. In fact, they discouraged any attempts to provide an ultimate fix, preferring to nibble around the edges and limit the damage of regulations but allow the incremental loss of property rights.

Their lobbyists and officials in Washington varied from refusing to work with my staff to actively discouraging us from putting forth this legislation.

They instead favored leaving the status quo alone and simply going after the new, even more far-reaching regulations being put forward by the EPA under President Obama. Their logic? They maintain that we would anger the environmentalists if we attempted to define "navigable waters." I responded that the environmental extremists who drive this debate already live in a constant state of angry emotionalism.

This tactical surrender was also supported by senior members of my caucus—the Old Guard—with an interest in these issues.

I was less than amused. The senior senators who were supposed to keep the EPA under control and the Washington representatives of the major effected industries were colluding to stop my bill.

Let me be clear. They weren't just quietly trying to persuade me from doing this. These big business interests and senior senators were actively and vocally undermining my efforts to help. I drew laughs in my caucus when I joked that even though Senator So-and-so was actively opposing my Defense of Property bill, I would actively support his incrementalist approach, as I did not see them as mutually exclusive.

I spent the better part of six months trying to work with all sides here, offering to craft specific legislative language. Admitting that perhaps others who had been dealing with these issues longer might have something to add to the solution, I repeatedly attempted to engage them on how to better the bill.

Finally, growing frustrated and sensing that those involved thus far really did not want to fully fix the problem, I let it be known before leaving Capitol Hill at the end of one week that I would be introducing this legislation when Congress resumed the following week.

I was immediately summoned to a meeting. This meeting involved a senior Republican senator with an interest in the wetlands issue. It also involved the lobbyists for nearly a dozen interest groups. I already had the support of many of the members these groups purported to represent here, but I was in for a surprise.

I was basically told to sit down and shut up. Industry was not interested in fighting the battle, I was told. This particular senior senator told me there was no point, that we would lose.

The Old Guard and the Beseechers sensed someone messing with their turf.

I was having none of it. In fact, it just made me more sure what I was doing was right, and more determined to take this battle forward.

I left the room and immediately began making phone calls. I called some of the major dues-paying CEOs of the national groups. They were astounded at what their supposed representatives were doing.

I called the state chapters—many of whom I knew to be on my side—to urge them to go on record with their support, to shame their national groups into action.

Outside groups like the American Land Rights Association and FreedomWorks began what I expect to be a long battle for support for my bill.

When an agency gets as out of control as the EPA has become, it is madness to simply allow the damage it has done for thirty years to stand. Waiting around to perhaps fight the EPA when they make another bad move is not exactly a prudent or productive strategy.

Yet this is exactly what the Old Guard and the Beseechers wanted to do.

In the end, I am reminded that those who make a living in Washington peddling influence rarely want to see major change. Change is the enemy of the entrenched establishment, be it the Tea Party challenging the big-spending Republicans, or liberty activists challenging the corporate welfare of Washington.

The battle for this bill will go on. John Rapanos fought for over twenty years. Mike and Chantell Sackett have been fighting for nearly fifteen years. Robert Lucas has rotted in jail for ten years and his eighty-year-old engineer suffers the same fate. I just arrived in Congress last year, but it is clear to me that what they were up against wasn't just the EPA. It wasn't just the Army Corps of Engineers. It wasn't a Democratic regulator versus a Republican regulator. It was, and is, the most powerful Leviathan of all—the Establishment and all its inertia and bureaucracy combining to maintain the status quo.

If Americans demand change, the Establishment demands that they endure the status quo. If citizens stand up, the Establishment insists that they stand down. If we mouth our grievances, the Establishment will insist that we shut up.

But I, for one, will not watch quietly as unelected bureaucrats continue to bleed us of our freedoms. I will not remain quiet. I cannot. And I will fight until I have no voice left to fight.

PART 2

★ ★ ★

The Lacey Act—An Open License for Government Bullying

"HE has combined with others to subject us to a Jurisdiction foreign to our Constitution, and unacknowledged by our Laws...FOR transporting us beyond Seas to be tried for pretended Offences..."

—THE DECLARATION OF INDEPENDENCE'S GRIEVANCES AGAINST KING GEORGE III

8

Leave American Businesses Alone

"The best minds are not in government. If any were, business would steal them away."
—RONALD REAGAN

* ★ ★

When I first heard that federal agents had raided the Gibson Guitar Corporation brandishing automatic weapons and confiscating millions of dollars in merchandise, computers, and equipment—well, I was horrified. My horror turned into absolute disbelief when I heard what Gibson was actually being accused of: violating a *foreign* law. Astonishingly, the U.S. Justice Department was trying to hold Gibson executives criminally liable for this. Our government wanted to prosecute these private businessmen and throw them in jail.

I personally called the CEO of Gibson, Henry Juszkiewicz, and invited him to come to Capitol Hill to testify about his ordeal. Most CEOs would have declined, choosing instead to shield themselves from any possible trouble that could arise from speaking out. Facing possible criminal charges, most men in Mr. Juszkiewicz's position would have simply taken solace in the safety of their attorneys.

Not him.

Mr. Juszkiewicz showed up on Capitol Hill, without any attorney, and publicly told the story of what his own government was trying to do to him and to Gibson.

The details of the story are as bad as you might expect—but

as Mr. Juszkiewicz himself mentioned to me that day in Washington, at least *he* was big enough to fight back. The government can try to bully him and his company all they want, but Gibson can afford to hire an army of lawyers. The government can seize millions from Gibson—but Mr. Juszkiewicz has millions more.

But there are many more—hundreds if not thousands—of Americans who simply cannot afford to fight back against their own government. It is for these people, the countless hardworking, taxpaying citizens just trying to play by the rules and do what's right, that Mr. Juszkiewicz and I fight this battle.

The Lacey Act is a frightening example of our government criminalizing activity that really shouldn't be criminal. David McNab and Abner Schoenwetter are victims of the Lacey Act who spent years in federal prison for "violating" invalid Honduran fishing regulations. Even Honduras's government insisted that they did not want these businessmen imprisoned—yet this did not deter the U.S. government from doing it anyway.

This is insane. We've lost our way.

The Lacey Act is a primary example of the infuriating tyranny that typically accompanies government expansion. The original intent was conservation—to prohibit trafficking in "illegal" wildlife, fish, and plants. The act was first signed into law in 1900, and has had subsequent amendments (in 1935, 1969, 1981, 1988, and most recently in 2008).

Legal scholars seem to agree that the end result of this act is an extremely broad law that contains harsh criminal penalties for the vaguest of reasons. The original maximum penalty for violating the Lacey Act was a $200 fine. No imprisonment was envisioned for such violations. But mere $200 fines don't make legislators seem "tough on crime," apparently, even if the "crime" amounts to bickering over the size of a lobster tail (the difference between four and six ounces can be a major criminal offense).

The Lacey Act's broad and unspecific delegation of congressional power to foreign governments runs completely afoul of Article I of the Constitution, which vests all legislative powers in the United States Congress.

It also runs afoul of common sense. Try explaining to any American that they could go to jail simply for buying or selling a product that is illegal under foreign law—not U.S. law. Try explaining to them that it wouldn't really matter if they were aware they were breaking these laws or not.

Of course, most Americans would look at you like you'd lost your mind. This is exactly how we should be looking at our government right now—like it has lost its mind.

It would be easy for a conservative Republican to look at the most recent high-profile Lacey Act atrocity—the action taken against Gibson—and see an overzealous Obama administration at fault. There's some merit to this. The Gibson case began under the Obama administration. The first raid was in 2009 and the second was in 2011.

But if you look deeper, the problem isn't as simple as an overly aggressive Obama administration. It is similar to what causes so many of the other problems in our government—the U.S. Congress.

The Lacey Act amendments that passed in 2008 are at the root of Gibson's struggle. And they are, once again, examples of our myriad of problems in Washington.

First, these amendments were not passed as a stand-alone bill. Two of the reforms I have advocated in Congress—"Read the Bills" and "One Subject at a Time"—would have likely stopped these amendments from ever passing.

You see, the 2008 additions to the Lacey Act were passed as part of the multiyear gigantic farm bill. What problem, exactly, were these changes trying to solve?

Deforestation in Malaysia.

I'll pause while you wonder why Congress was thinking for even one nanosecond that it either needs to address or somehow could impact deforestation in Malaysia.

Still, there was our Congress, international busybodies at work. While most Americans are worried about trillion-dollar deficits, a health care crisis, and a crumbling infrastructure, in 2008 our illustrious Capitol Hill leaders were more concerned with Malaysian deforestation.

Rosewood and ebony, two of the most prized woods for making quality guitar fretboards, are found in Malaysian forests. But the guitar manufacturers of the world—Gibson only being one of them—are responsible for barely 5 percent of the consumption of Malaysian rosewood and ebony. So what accounts for the other 95 percent? Who, or what, is the primary culprit (if there is one) in the destruction of Malaysian forests?

Wealthy Chinese, who use this wood for furniture.

For some reason we will probably never really know, the U.S. Congress is interested in fixing an alleged problem in Malaysian forests. So they pass a law that even at its best hope of success would only fix 5 percent of the problem—leaving the Chinese to do whatever damage they like with the other 95 percent.

American jobs will be lost. Americans will be left scratching their heads, wondering how these legislators even managed to get into high office in the first place. Let's not leave out that this amendment to the Lacey Act passed under the Bush administration, not President Obama's.

Now we are left trying to fix the problem.

To explain the Lacey Act a bit more, I'm going to tell you three horror stories—that of Gibson, that of some Honduran fishermen, and that of a Kentucky family harvesting "caviar" from fish in the Ohio River. These stories will shock you, anger you, and, hopefully, motivate you to join the fight to restore sanity to our country's laws.

9

★ ★ ★

Stringing Up Gibson Guitar

" 'The godfather of rock 'n' roll,' I call him. Without him, none of us would have a job."
—BON JOVI GUITARIST RICHIE SAMBORA ON
GIBSON GUITAR LEGEND LES PAUL

* * *

There are few American companies so ingrained in our popular history and our national culture as Gibson Guitar Corporation. So many artists for so many years have done what Bruce Springsteen once sang—they picked up a guitar, and they learned how to make it talk. Talk to us. Talk for us. Talk about us. Talk about our lives, our dreams, our hopes, our fears.

The history of Gibson guitars is the history of America in the twentieth century. From jazz, to blues, to country, to rock and roll, Gibson has been a major part of what many have long considered America's most popular export—music.

At the turn of the century, Gibson began by making mandolins, changing those instruments' shape and tone and by the 1920s becoming known as the maker of the best bluegrass mandolins in the world, a musical genre with deep roots in my home state of Kentucky.

A few decades later, Gibson made some of the most popular acoustic guitars of the pre- and postwar eras. Musicians popularized the Gibson acoustic guitar in country music, and it is widely considered to be the most important guitar in country music history.

Gibson's biggest claim to fame, and most lasting overall contribution to music, is the introduction of the Les Paul model electric guitar. Gibson did not invent the electric guitar, but it is credited with having one of the first commercially successful models.

The Les Paul is iconic, instantly recognizable by sight and sound to music fans across the globe. It is so thoroughly associated with Gibson that we asked the company to bring or send a Les Paul to our Senate hearing where Gibson CEO Henry Juszkiewicz would testify back in 2011.

We ran into a snag, though. It seems that the frugal CEO was not planning on doing what most CEOs do when they travel. He was not flying on a private jet from Nashville to Washington. No, instead, the head of Gibson flew into Washington, D.C., on Southwest Airlines. This saved their company at least $5,000. Remember this the next time someone—an American president, for example—lumps "greedy" corporate CEOs all together, criticizing them for using "private jets."

In any case, the guitar wouldn't fit in the overhead bins of the airline, and I think we can all understand why Gibson was reluctant to have their CEO check a $4,000 electric guitar as baggage. Instead, Gibson shipped the Les Paul to my Senate office. It arrived the morning of the hearing, with strict instructions not to touch or play it, but to leave it at the hearing for Mr. Juszkiewicz to open and display.

Arriving at the hearing, my chief of staff Doug Stafford, who is a guitar player, noted to Mr. Juszkiewicz his admiration for this beautiful guitar. He explained how he had always wanted to own a Les Paul. Mr. Juszkiewicz just smiled and asked knowingly, "You played the guitar, didn't you?" Of course, Doug had. No guitar player could have resisted, he told Mr. Juszkiewicz, who politely smiled and agreed.

Mr. Juszkiewicz's testimony at the hearing that day was

important for two primary reasons. First, his story desperately needed to be told, and I will tell it to you here. But second, it was important that a company with the financial and legal means to fight our government actually did so. Too often corporate and government interests are either in cahoots from the beginning, or, if pressed, the corporate interest will take the path of least resistance and make some kind of a deal. In corporations' typical efforts to get any legal troubles behind them, the same bad laws and regulations that led to those troubles are also left in place.

Not Gibson. Their CEO was going to stand and fight for his company's rights.

And here's what happened to them.

The first problem arose in 2009. Gibson executives were holding a corporate meeting when Mr. Juszkiewicz received a phone call that the Department of Homeland Security was raiding his factory in Nashville. His first reaction was that this had to be some kind of a joke. "I make *guitars*," he recalled thinking at the time. What kind of terrorist threat or home-land security issue could possibly involve guitars?

Then, as more information began coming in, the reports of the raid became more detailed. There were more than thirty armed agents in his factory. They had been sent as a SWAT team, with automatic weapons, bulletproof vests, and all the rest. The agents evacuated the entire factory, forcing out nearly three hundred employees, who at this point were very scared and confused. Workers remember being shocked and befuddled, wondering what could have possibly warranted such an intrusive display of firepower.

The feds seized hundreds of thousands of dollars' worth of raw materials, including woods from Madagascar and India, these being the source of the "problem." Mr. Juszkiewicz didn't yet know this yet. There's no way he could have known. When he arrived at the scene to ask just what in the heck the government thought it was doing, he was told that the information was "sealed."

Sealed search warrants do exist. They are even occasionally necessary in putting together certain criminal cases against the largest crime organizations. But last I checked, Gibson was not a large crime organization. Still, try telling that to the federal government. The agents sent the workers home. They seized the raw materials. They essentially shut down factory production, costing the company millions of dollars. Worse, the government gave Gibson no answers and continued to stonewall. The government filed no charges. In fact, it was months before Gibson even knew why they had been raided or even knew it was the wood the government was looking for.

Desperate for a day in court to prove their innocence and recover their lost materials, Gibson sued the U.S. government. Ask yourself this: When was the last time someone under investigation for a major federal crime had to sue the government to get into court? If Gibson were actually guilty, it would seem the party urging a speedy prosecution would be the government. As of 2012, this case is still in court, because the government asked for a delay in the lawsuit.

At the time, what it appeared the government was (unsuccessfully) trying to prove was that Gibson had imported woods from Madagascar and India that were protected. This was patently false, and provably so.

Gibson had supplied the government with eighty thousand pages of material in response to the investigation. The company had even provided—at government request—the sales receipt of every guitar sold during that period. That's right—

even those who purchased guitars from Gibson might not be safe. Still, no charges were filed. No resolution was reached. Gibson simply sat in limbo for two years, unable to prove their case or recover their materials.

But the government was not done with them. The raid in 2009 was in one location and limited to raw materials. Then came a second raid—on three different facilities.

Another armed federal SWAT team descended upon Gibson's Nashville and Memphis offices and production facilities. Agents brandishing automatic weapons ordered Gibson's luthiers to put down their tools, move away from their computers, lay aside the wood and strings, and let the government in—to harass them.

What heinous crime had brought the wrath of Big Brother down upon this quiet Nashville guitar factory a second time? Was it a drug bust? Had Gibson been smuggling drugs in the hollow-body guitars? Or was it a murder or a kidnapping?

A closer inspection of the federal badges by the workers and management of Gibson revealed the letters "FW." FW? What federal law enforcement agency was this? Fish and Wildlife. I'm not joking. Agents with bad attitudes and automatic weapons had barraged into Gibson from . . . the Fish and Wildlife Service. I wish I were making this up.

The craftsmen and workers watched in disbelief as the agents stated their reason for the armed assault. Gibson had been accused of violating the Lacey Act. Though you, the reader, now know what the Lacey Act is, Gibson employees could certainly be forgiven if their reaction had been "we violated *what*, exactly?"

I know this sounds like a bad joke or outlandish made-for-TV movie. I assure you, this is no laughing matter. The

Lacey Act—far beyond its original intention—now demands massive fines and even jail time. This case involved countless lawyers, endless defense, and years in court.

Under the Lacey Act, guitar players everywhere could find themselves in hot water with the feds too. You see, for the government to succeed in prosecuting Gibson, it will have to prove that the guitars made and sold in this country were made illegally. This would make Gibson guitar owners nation-wide open to prosecution as well.

I'm still not kidding.

As Gibson's CEO explained, the government was accusing his company of breaking a law that says that Indian wood products must be "improved" before being exported. "Improved" means they must be manufactured in India.

Our Justice Department was bullying an American company for importing wood and then hiring American citizens to work with it. The Justice Department even put this all in writing, maintaining that if Gibson would just ship the "improving" wood jobs overseas, then everything would be okay. Let me be clear—our government was saying that if the skilled workers at Gibson were to simply surrender that work instead to Indian woodworkers, then the Lacey Act complaint would go away.

Mr. Juszkiewicz wants to make sure he is very clear on this matter. He is a lifelong conservationist. His company complies with laws regarding conservation, even though, as mentioned, Gibson consumes a very small amount of raw materials.

In fact, the wood seized in the second raid was controlled by the Forest Stewardship Council. According to Juszkie-wicz, "Gibson has a long history of supporting sustainable and responsible sources of wood, and has worked diligently with entities such as the Rainforest Alliance and Greenpeace to secure Forest Stewardship Council–certified supplies. The wood seized on August 24 satisfied FSC standards." Gibson has never been tried for anything. The first raid, ostensibly about the raw materials violations, has never been prosecuted.

Interestingly, the U.S. government is claiming to be enforcing the laws of Madagascar and India. But if that is true, they should tell the governments of Madagascar and India.

Both countries have said in writing that Gibson has not broken any of their laws. In every shipment, Gibson had clearance from both foreign and U.S. customs, following all the rules and paying all the necessary tariffs. These foreign governments certify all of this. Our U.S. Customs confirms this to be true. But the U.S. government doesn't recognize any of this and still proceeds with its vendetta against Gibson.

Why?

Could it be that the main competitor of Gibson, Fender Musical Instrument Corporation, is a huge Democratic Party donor? When Henry Juszkiewicz is asked that question, he demurs, shrugs, and says, "Could be." Obviously, this would be hard to prove. In a strange way, it would almost be comforting if this vendetta against Gibson were nothing more than just basic corruption and petty partisan politics. At least at some detestable level, it would have a sort of logic to it.

The alternative is worse—that our government really is just this stupid.

10

★ ★ ★

Trapping Lobster Fishermen

"Government, even in its best state, is but a necessary evil; in its worst state, an intolerable one."
—THOMAS PAINE

$\star \ \star \ \star$

At this point it should not surprise readers of this book that your federal government has a definite, firm, and nonnegotiable position on the subject of…lobster tails. They have mandatory sizes. They have regulations on whether they were young or old, egg-bearing or not. They even care about whether those lobsters were packaged in plastic bags or cardboard boxes.

Actually, to be fair to our government, these are not U.S. regulations. They are regulations thought up by the government of Honduras. Let's discuss two important facts about this matter up front:

First, the government of Honduras actually cares about the size, delivery, and packaging of lobster tails. I suppose it should make us feel somewhat better that inane regulations are not the sole prerogative of the U.S. government—but only a little better. You would think such overregulation would reflect "first-world problems." In other words, America is free (the examples of government abuse in this book notwithstanding), prosperous, and successful. We feed and clothe ourselves, have shelter, provide education, and generally are able to take care of ourselves, so therefore we can afford to worry about the size of lobster tails.

But what about Honduras? Honduras is the second poorest country in Central America, and the third poorest in all of Latin America. Honduras has real poverty, not "why won't the government pay for the data plan on my cell phone" kind of poverty. Honduran poverty is tragic—malnutrition, starvation, and oppression. Hondurans live on an average income of $1,800 per year. That much per *month* would qualify as poor in the United States.

Honduras is not exactly politically stable. Their last coup was in 2009, in which President Manuel Zelaya was overthrown, due mostly to public frustration over his administration's inability to address widespread poverty.

With this awful national backdrop, the Honduran government, with all of these problems, busied itself making rules about lobster tail size—and the U.S. government, at great expense, was hell-bent on enforcing them.

Four businessmen were involved in the Honduran fishermen case. All four of them, three Americans and one Honduran citizen, were sent to prison for alleged violations of the Lacey Act, in an attempt by our government to enforce foreign laws. Similar to the Gibson case, the foreign country under consideration really didn't want the United States to prosecute, and in fact had asked our federal government not to do so in a U.S. court.

With Gibson, the Indian and Madagascar governments argued that the company had unquestionably complied with the law. The Honduran fishermen case wasn't quite as clear. The Honduran government, including the attorney general for their country, insisted that the law under which the United States is prosecuting is invalid because it never was properly executed or signed into Honduran law.

But before we get to the conclusion, let's tell the story.

In 1999, the National Marine Fisheries Service received an anonymous tip about undersized lobster tails being shipped from Honduras to Alabama by Honduran businessman David McNab.

I'm sorry, it may be wrong, but I can't type that sentence without laughing out loud. Go ahead, read it again, and see if you can without shaking your head in bewilderment. It's comical. I even wondered if the National Marine Fisheries Service in this story was somehow part of the Fish and Wildlife Service that Gibson had to tangle with.

But they aren't the same agency. They aren't even under the same agency. They're not even in the same cabinet department. One is in the Department of the Interior, one is in the Department of Commerce (both of which I proposed we eliminate in my Fiscal Year 2012 Budget, I'm proud to say).

Why are there two similar departments? What do both of them do? After investigating, I must tell you, I still have no idea. Here is the official government description. See if you can figure it out:

> The U.S. Fish and Wildlife Service is the principal Federal agency responsible for conserving, protecting and enhancing fish, wildlife and plants and their habitats for the continuing benefit of the American people. The agency enforces Federal wildlife laws, administers the Endangered Species Act, manages migratory bird populations, restores nationally significant fisheries, conserves and restores wildlife habitat such as wetlands, and helps foreign governments with their conservation efforts.

And:

> The National Marine Fisheries Service is the principal steward of the nation's living marine resources, protecting marine and anadromous species under the Endangered Species Act and the Marine Mammal Protection Act.

Back to the story. Though I'm still curious, I am going to ignore any exploration of why this anonymous tip might have occurred. Yet once it did, agents from the NMFS detained the ship from Honduras as it arrived in Alabama. Characteristic of these agencies, the owners were not given an explanation of what the problems were. Weeks went by, but still no word as the NMFS continued to hold the ship and its seventy thousand pounds of lobster.

This wasn't guitar wood here. We're talking about freshly caught seafood. The very act of holding it for weeks with no explanation likely destroyed it. But no matter—the government was just getting started.

The lobster was soon offloaded and sent to a government freezer in Florida. Now, I ask you, why does our government have a freezer, waiting and ready, capable of holding seventy thousand pounds of lobster?

For months, the lobster stayed in Florida. The fishermen/businessmen sat in their offices wondering what the government was doing. As it turned out, the government had been spending this time desperately trying to find Honduran laws under which to prosecute the fishermen.

After numerous phone calls, letters, and trips to Honduras, the NMFS focused on three provisions. The first details the processing and packaging of fish harvested in Honduran waters. This 1993 regulation, promulgated pursuant to a 1973 statute, included the mention of packaging in cardboard boxes. The second regulation prohibits harvesting any lobsters with tails shorter than 5.5 inches. This must have surprised the NMFS agents, since the market price lists published by NMFS include prices for two- and three-ounce Caribbean spiny lobsters from Honduras. A government expert acknowledged at trial that these little lobsters would all have tails shorter than 5.5 inches. The third Honduran provision prohibits destroying or harvesting "eggs, or the offspring of fish, chelonians or other aquatic species for profit."

Six months after sending them to the cooler, NMFS agents finally began to inspect the locked-up lobster tails. Only about 3 percent of the lobster tails turned out to be less than 5.5 inches long. Just 7 percent showed any evidence of having been egg-bearing lobsters. These small amounts belie the suggestion that David McNab or his employees were intentionally harvesting young or egg-bearing lobsters. Nevertheless, prosecutors included these regulations as predicates for alleged violations of the Lacey Act.

Charges based on the size and egg-harvesting regulations would only allow NMFS to seize the small portions of lobster tails that were under 5.5 inches or showed evidence of bearing eggs. This apparently was not enough. Because all the lobsters were in clear plastic bags instead of cardboard boxes, the government declared the entire shipment illegal and formally seized all seventy thousand pounds of lobster tails.

Government prosecutors, not satisfied even with thirty-five tons of lobster, filed criminal charges against McNab. They also charged three American businesspeople, Robert

Blandford, Abbie Schoenwetter, and Diane Huang, who frequently purchased and distributed lobster tails from McNab. All charges against McNab, and most charges against the others, were predicated on the three Honduran regulations applied through the Lacey Act. No charges against the defendants were ever brought in Honduras. The alleged Lacey Act violations served primarily to trigger more serious charges. If importing the lobster in bags instead of boxes was illegal, prosecutors reasoned, then planning to import it was criminal conspiracy, the actual importation was smuggling, and payments became felony money laundering.

At the district court's foreign law hearing, McNab presented copious evidence showing that the Honduran regulations in question were invalid. No size restriction had ever been signed by the president of Honduras, an absolute requirement for such a regulation under Honduran law. The attorney general of Honduras supplied an opinion, confirming other testimony, that because the size restriction was not signed into law it did not have the force of law.

McNab presented other witnesses, including a former Honduran minister of justice, who testified that the egg-harvesting regulation was never intended to apply to animals that happened to bear eggs when caught. The prohibition against harvesting or destroying eggs for profit was meant to do just that, to prevent the harvesting of eggs themselves (turtle eggs in particular).

Government prosecutors somehow convinced the court to ignore McNab's extensive evidence and instead accept the testimony of a single midlevel Honduran bureaucrat, Liliana Paz. For reasons that remain unexplained, the "secretary-general" of the Honduran Ministry of Agriculture and Livestock—an official whose primary duty is to be "an instrument of communication" and who has no expertise or authority to render legal opinions—testified that all the regulations were valid and had the force of law.

Despite the obvious lack of criminal intent on the part of the defendants, as well as concerns about the validity of the Honduran regulations, all four businesspeople were convicted on a general verdict. In August 2001, McNab, Blandford, and Schoenwetter were each sentenced to eight years in prison. Huang, a businesswoman from New Jersey who resold seafood to restaurants like Red Lobster, was sentenced to two years in prison.

The government trumpeted the convictions in press releases that labeled McNab "the ringleader of a smuggling operation." The reports misled the public by suggesting that McNab was intentionally harvesting undersized and egg-bearing lobsters, never mentioning that these were a negligible portion of his catch. The government failed to note that the only reason for declaring the entire shipment illegal was that it was packed in bags, not boxes. In effect, the defendants were convicted of smuggling because they packed lobster in clear plastic bags instead of opaque cardboard boxes.

A press release issued by the National Oceanic and Atmospheric Administration, the agency that includes the NMFS, implied that McNab's business success was part of his wrongdoing. NOAA pointed out that McNab owns a "fleet of vessels, each of which can deploy thousands of lobster traps," as if this in itself is somehow a wrongful act. Striking an even more bizarre note, NOAA declared, "The wealth from McNab's

vast harvest was denied to the common citizens of Honduras."
McNab, a Honduran citizen, is apparently not "common"
enough for the Sandinistas at NOAA.

After sentencing, the court was prepared to allow all four
defendants to remain free pending their appeals. Federal
prosecutors objected to allowing a foreigner like McNab
to remain free on bond and the Eleventh Circuit Court of
Appeals sent him to prison. McNab is now in his fourth year
of incarceration.

On appeal before the Eleventh Circuit, two of the three
appellate judges effectively declared Honduras a banana repub-
lic, unfit to construe its own laws. The court decided that it
would be unwise to disagree with the prosecutors' interpretation of these foreign laws. Basically, our government was saying that anything that the Honduran government said wasn't
worth listening to. This ignored the holdings of other circuits
and the proper role of appellate courts in general. Even worse,
the two judges asserted that Honduran officials could not be
trusted because they might be bribed or manipulated. Somehow this failed to undermine the credibility of Ms. Paz, the
midlevel Honduran bureaucrat who testified for the prosecution. In the interest of "finality," the court of appeals upheld the
lower court on every issue, no doubt because if just one of the three
Honduran regulations was found to be invalid, all of the convictions would fail.

The decision of the Eleventh Circuit is only more troubling when considered in light of the critical new evidence that
emerged from Honduras during and after the trial. After the
foreign law hearing, McNab had filed an action in the Honduran Court of First Instance of Administrative Law challenging
the size restriction. Several months after the end of the crimi-

nal trial, the Honduran court formally held that the size limit was void and declared that it had never had the force of law.

McNab's attorneys also discovered that the law authorizing the packaging regulations was repealed in 1995. Under Honduran law, a regulation is automatically repealed when the authorizing statute is repealed. Even the prosecution's witness from the Honduran Ministry of Agriculture and Livestock admitted this in an affidavit. It also became clear that the egg-harvesting provision had been repealed in a way that, under Honduran law, operated retroactively.

McNab additionally filed a motion before the Honduran national human rights commissioner challenging Ms. Paz's testimony about Honduran law. The commissioner, Dr. Leo Valladares, is an internationally respected constitutional lawyer and human rights advocate. His office in Honduras is charged with addressing complaints that government officials' actions constitute "legal error." Dr. Valladares issued a report, which the minister of agriculture signed, stating that Ms. Paz's testimony constituted "an error of law." The scholarly report found that the packaging regulation was repealed in 1995, the size restriction had "never had the force of law," and that the egg-bearing provision had been retroactively repealed.

The government of Honduras, through its embassy, directed all of this information to the U.S. State Department, asking that they forward it directly to the Department of Justice. The attorney general of Honduras also filed an amicus curiae brief with the Eleventh Circuit, providing this information and explaining that McNab and the other businesspeople had not violated any Honduran law. All of this was ignored by the court of appeals when it concluded that "finality" was apparently more important than justice.

How could this happen? What kind of a "justice" system is this?

The prosecution of four businesspeople for normal business activities highlights the dangerous but growing trend in our government to expand criminal liability against normal social and economic conduct. Historically, a criminal conviction required proof of criminal intent (mens rea, a "guilty mind") in addition to the wrongful infliction of harm (actus reus, a "bad act"). Even if the Honduran statutes had not turned out to be uniformly invalid, there was never any evidence that showed the businesspeople acted with criminal intent. Rather the evidence seems to prove that they were simply engaged in catching and selling seafood in a way that any businessperson would consider lawful.

This prosecution also reveals the risks of federalizing criminal law. Observers have long warned against allowing the federal government to encroach on the traditional state function of enacting and enforcing general criminal laws. Here, the federal government, through the Lacey Act, claims to enforce foreign laws against foreign and U.S. citizens. These regulations were not made by the U.S. Congress or by some executive agency, but by a foreign government with unfamiliar procedures. If the government of Honduras had actually believed these regulations to be valid, they were free to bring charges. Instead, the U.S. government prosecuted a case on what turned out to be bad law.

Each of the four defendants was trying only to earn a living through normal commercial activity when an anonymous accusatory fax sent the U.S. government to destroy their lives. This ordeal has been happening for over a decade. David

McNab waits in prison to see if his appeal to the court of last resort will even take the case. The three American business-people, Robert Blandford, Abbie Schoenwetter, and Diane Huang, wait anxiously for the decision that could save them— or send them to prison for years.

11

★ ★ ★

Bureaucrats Destroy Caviar Dreams

"If the law supposes that... then the law is an ass, an idiot."

—MR. BUMBLE IN *OLIVER TWIST*

* ★ ★

On January 17, 2012, Steven and Cornelia Joyce Kinder, owners of Kinder Caviar and Black Star Caviar Company, pled guilty in their federal case of harvesting paddlefish. The Justice Department's plea agreement stated that both Steve Kinder and Cornelia Joyce Kinder admitted to aiding and abetting one another in harvesting the fish. The agreement stated that they should have known these paddlefish were harvested in Ohio waters in violation of state law, through the use of gill nets attached to the Ohio shoreline. This happened on or about May 5, 2007, and thereafter the Kinders had transported the paddlefish to Kentucky with the intent to sell them.

Now, if you're like me, obviously we are getting down on our hands and knees to thank our federal government for addressing this pressing matter. But it gets even more ridiculous. As part of a plea agreement, both Kinder Caviar and Black Star Caviar Company have each agreed to pay a $5,000 fine and serve a three-year term of probation, during which time those companies will be prohibited from applying for or receiving a CITES Export Permit.

Additionally, Steve and Cornelia Joyce Kinder have agreed to serve a three-year term of probation, during which time they will each perform one hundred hours of community service, be prohibited from fishing anywhere in the Ohio River, where that river forms the border between Ohio and Kentucky, and be prohibited from applying for or receiving a CITES Export Permit, either on behalf of themselves or anyone else. In accordance with Kentucky law, the Kinders also face possible suspension of their Kentucky commercial fishing licenses. Finally, as part of the plea agreement, the boat and truck that were used in furtherance of the Lacey Act crimes have been forfeited.

So to recap, the Kinders may or may not have broken a law about which fish can be harvested in which water, a law, by the way, that differs from one side of the river between Kentucky and Ohio to the other. Not to mention the fact that, historically, the river is actually controlled by Kentucky, not Ohio. If the Kinders had hung their nets from the Kentucky bank and not the Ohio side, their fishing would not have been questioned.

To punish this heinous caviar crime, they have to pay fines, give up their livelihood, surrender their property, and be publicly branded as criminals. The government treated them as if they had just held up a bank.

As you might imagine, this isn't the whole story, but even if it were, I think I would still be outraged.

I met Joyce and Steven on more than one occasion in northern Kentucky, near where their business is based. Joyce approached me at a political picnic when I was running for the Senate. She beamed from ear to ear as she described in exciting detail her new caviar business. I even tasted the caviar they were harvesting. I hope that wasn't also a crime. I think I might have even carried some of their caviar across states lines—will the federal government come after me next?

Joyce and Steve Kinder are good and decent people, just trying to earn a living. When we first met, they were also active in the Tea Party, trying to take back our country. The Kinders thought the government was out of control based on the bank bailouts, Obamacare, and trillion-dollar deficits alone. They could not have fathomed the kind of tyranny our federal government was capable of, and the misery it was about to visit upon them—a husband-and-wife small business team.

In 2011, the Justice Department came after the Kinders, saying they were in violation of the Lacey Act, which we've described in other chapters. The act is supposed to address or regulate how fish and wildlife are caught, imported, or exported.

We have a trillion-dollar deficit hole in our budget. We have bridges literally falling down and an infrastructure that is crumbling. We have a military that is stretched entirely too thin. We have a broken entitlement system, and a bunch of Washington "leaders" too scared or inept to do anything about it.

We have a border so porous that illegal immigrants and terrorists alike could be coming across it at any moment. We are told it cannot be fixed because we don't have the manpower.

Yet somehow, some way, we have the manpower and resources to prosecute people for the following *major* "crimes":

- Illegally harvesting paddlefish from Ohio and false reporting to the Kentucky Department of Fish and Wildlife Resources.
- Providing false information about the paddlefish eggs to the U.S. Fish and Wildlife Service in order to obtain permits to export the paddlefish eggs to foreign customers, including the quantity of paddlefish eggs to be exported; the names of the fishermen who harvested the paddlefish; and the location where the paddlefish were harvested.

It would be funny if it weren't so tragic. While the above statement itself seems comical because it is so illogical, it is serious—each count included a maximum fine of $250,000 and five years in jail. Per company.

So the Kinders were facing the prospect of decades in jail and millions in fines. For doing something the government didn't like—harvesting eggs from paddlefish.

I don't even know which direction to go in telling this story because it is so utterly ridiculous. The Kinders fought the government for a while, but realized that they were in an impossible position and accepted the guilty plea to avoid prison time and total financial ruin. It is hard to blame them in this situation.

It's not as if the Kinders were operating in secret, trying to do something illegal under everyone's nose. They were a well-known, and, at least they thought, well-respected company. Their company was featured on the Kentucky Department of Agriculture's website, whose blurb for them reads:

> Caspian Sea style caviar made right here in the Bluegrass! American caviar now comparable to the caviars of the Caspian Sea!
>
> [A]s the catch and quotas of Caspian Sea caviar continue to decline, prices will steadily increase. Kinder Caviar is fast becoming the choice for the caviar savvy connoisseur.

Knowing that, and knowing the Kinders, I sought them out to discuss their case for this book and for my own information.

That proved to be more difficult than I thought. You see, the government nearly drove the Kinders into hiding. Even though we had many mutual friends, it took weeks to locate and contact Joyce and Steve Kinder, who were staying with friends in a different area of Kentucky than where they're from.

They were scared of their own government.

This is what our government is doing to good and decent men and women just trying to earn a living. Government bullies, indeed.

12

★ ★ ★

How Can We Solve
the Problem?

"Bad laws are the worst sort of tyranny."
—EDMUND BURKE

∗ ∗ ∗

The overcriminalization of commerce and general business activity through the Lacey Act has created exactly what concerned Justice Scalia, an increase in the volume of "imprecise laws"—laws that can mean virtually anything, at any given time, depending on the government-agency bureaucrat you're unlucky enough to speak to or even unluckier to be targeted by. Americans shouldn't be treated like this.

This year, I introduced the Freedom from Over-Criminalization and Unjust Seizures Act (FOCUS Act) to address these issues, cosponsored by Congressman Paul Broun of Georgia. I said during my testimony when introducing the FOCUS Act on May 8, 2012:

> Congressman Broun and I introduced companion bills in the Senate and in the House because of our shared concern regarding a dangerous law called the Lacey Act. The FOCUS Act makes significant revisions to the Lacey Act, revisions that we believe are necessary to prevent Americans from having their businesses raided by armed federal agents, their property seized, and even being sent to federal prison.

I refer to the Lacey Act as "dangerous" because of the ways in which it has already wreaked havoc in the lives of many innocent Americans. The Lacey Act serves as a high profile and frightening example of over-criminalization. Victims include Abner Schoenwetter and David McNab, who spent years in federal prison for "violating" Honduran fishing regulations that the Honduran government itself argued were invalid.

Most recently, just this past August, Henry Juszkiewicz, the Chairman and CEO of Gibson Guitar Corporation, had his company raided by armed federal agents. A half million dollars' worth of Mr. Juszkiewicz's property was seized, along with guitars and computer hard drives. His factory was shut down for a day, and his employees were ordered to go home. All this was done to him because he allegedly violated the Lacey Act, yet the Department of Justice has yet to file any formal charges against him.

In my testimony today, I will first provide a brief background regarding the history of the Lacey Act. I will then discuss the ways in which I believe this law violates the original intent of the Constitution, and will summarize the revisions the FOCUS Act makes to the Lacey Act. I will conclude with a discussion of the manner in which the FOCUS Act relates to my overall concern with the ever-growing threat of overcriminalization.

I. Background

The Lacey Act is a conservation law that attempts to prohibit trafficking in "illegal" wildlife, fish and plants. The original law was passed in 1900 for the purpose of protecting against interstate poaching. Congress later amended and expanded the Lacey Act to make it a crime to import or take any wildlife, fish, or plants "in violation of any foreign law." Since its passage in 1900, subsequent amendments (in 1935, 1969, 1981, 1988, and most recently 2008) have produced what today is an extremely broad and vague law that contains harsh criminal penalties.

As Paul Larkin, senior legal fellow at the Heritage Foundation explains, "The Lacey Act would not raise concern if the only penalty were a civil fine, but the law authorizes up to one year's imprisonment for every violation of the act. A one-year term of confinement may not seem onerous (unless, of course, you have to serve it), but a combination of one-year sentences could add up quickly. For example, if each fish taken in violation of the act were to constitute a separate offense, a fisherman could wind up with a three- or four-figure term of imprisonment just by bringing aboard one net's worth of fish."

Notably, the original Lacey Act of 1900 contained a penalty "not exceeding two hundred dollars," and there was no provision imposing jail or prison time. When the Lacey Act was significantly amended in 1981—an amendment that expanded the potential penalties to allow for felony criminal convictions—a representative of the National Rifle Association specifically voiced civil liberties concerns with the changes, stating that his "first concern [was] with the broad expansion of criminal liability."

II. The Lacey Act Is Unconstitutional

I believe that the Lacey Act in its current form violates our Constitution in a couple of significant ways. First, its broad and unspecific delegation of congressional power to foreign governments violates Article I of the Constitution, which vests all legislative powers in the United States Congress alone. By making it a federal offense to import fish, wildlife, or plants "in violation of any foreign law," Congress essentially delegates lawmaking authority to other nations.

Second, the Lacey Act is unconstitutionally vague, and fails to satisfy basic due process requirements of fair notice. As the Heritage Foundation notes, the Lacey Act in fact "violates one of the fundamental tenets of Anglo-American common law: that 'men of common intelligence' must be able to understand what a law means.... The criminal law must be clear not to the average lawyer, but to the average *person*. Even if there were lawyers who could readily answer intricate questions of foreign law—and do so for free—the criminal law is held to a higher standard."

Consider the practical effect of having a law such as the Lacey Act on the books that makes it a federal crime to violate any fish, wildlife, or plant law or regulation of any country in the world. The Heritage Foundation's Paul Larkin writes:

No one should be held accountable under this nation's law for violating a foreign nation's law. Laws come in all forms (e.g., statutes vs. regula-

tions); in all shapes and sizes (e.g., the Sherman Act vs. the Clean Air Act); and in all degrees of comprehensibility (e.g., the law of homicide vs. the Resource Conservation and Recovery Act). Different bodies have authority to promulgate laws (e.g., legislatures, courts, and agencies); to interpret them (e.g., the president or an agency's general counsel); and to enforce them (e.g., city, state, and federal law enforcement officers and prosecutors). And that is just in America.

Foreign nations may have very different allocations of governmental power, bureaucracies, and enforcement personnel. Some will speak and write in English; some will not. Some will make their decisions public; some will not. Some will have one entity that can speak authoritatively about its own laws; some will not. And different components of foreign governments may change their interpretations of their own laws over time, perhaps nullifying the effect of a prior interpretation, or perhaps not.

It is sheer lunacy to assume that the average citizen can keep track of such laws, let alone do so by him- or herself without a supporting cast of lawyers—that is, assuming that the average citizen could find a lawyer knowledgeable about the intricacies of a particular foreign nation's law.

A particularly tragic real-life example of the manner in which the Lacey Act violates basic constitutional requirements of due process and fair notice occurred with the convictions and imprisonment of Abner Schoenwetter and David McNab [in the previous chapter]. There are violent criminals who spend less time in prison than did these two innocent men.

The FOCUS Act would alter the Lacey Act by removing all references to "foreign law." It would also remove the Lacey Act's criminal penalties and substitute a reasonable civil penalty system. Lacey Act violations with a market value of less than $350 would be subject to a maximum penalty of $10,000, and other violations would be subject to a penalty of up to $200,000. These changes would remove the constitutional flaws inherent in the Lacey Act in its current form.

At this juncture I had explained not only the origins and subsequent misuse of the Lacey Act, but also that our Constitution doesn't give the federal government such authority to begin with. Washington leaders operate daily thinking they can simply do whatever they like, whether the Constitution they took an oath to uphold gives them the power to or not. The Lacey Act is but one small example.

But the immediate damaging effects of such law is unquestionably overcriminalization—where government bureaucrats blur the line between legal and illegal beyond any common-sense recognition. Normal, everyday business activity all of the sudden becomes a "crime." Or as I said during my testimony:

III. The Problem of Overcriminalization

The Lacey Act is but one example of the ever-growing problem of overcriminalization that we face in this country. Criminal law is increasingly being used as a tool by our government bureaucracies to punish and control honest businesspeople attempting to make a living. Historically, the criminal law was intended to punish only offenses that were known and understood by all people to be inherently evil or wrongful, offenses such as murder, rape, theft, arson, etc. Yet today the criminal law is constantly used to punish behavior such as fishing without a permit, packaging a product incorrectly, or shipping something with an "improper" label.

The plain language of our Constitution specifies a very limited number of federal crimes. But we have now moved so far away from the original intent of our Constitution that we don't even know or have a complete list of all the federal criminal laws on the books. There are over 4,450 federal statutory crimes scattered throughout the U.S. Code. And it is estimated that there are tens of thousands more crimes that exist among all our federal regulations. But no one—not even criminal law professors or criminal lawyers—actually knows the exact number with certainty.

In addition to not knowing the exact number of federal crimes, another serious problem is that many of the criminal statutes that have been passed by Congress in recent years lack adequate mens rea requirements. In other words, Congress passes laws that either completely lack—or have an extremely weak—"guilty mind" requirement, which means that someone charged under the statute could be convicted of a federal offense when he or she simply made an honest mistake, or did not possess the criminal culpability traditionally necessary for a criminal conviction.

The Lacey Act is a frightening example of this trend of overcriminalization. I urge my colleagues to support Congressman Broun and me in our efforts to pass the FOCUS Act. As Justice Scalia recently stated, "We face a Congress that puts forth an ever-increasing volume of laws in general, and of criminal laws in particular. It should be no surprise that as the volume increases, so do the number of imprecise laws.... In the field of criminal law, at least, it is time to call a halt."

Though introduced on its own and through the amendment process, the FOCUS Act has yet to become law. The bill has made it through at least one committee process in the House, but Senate Democrats refused to vote on it when I last proposed it in June 2012. Regardless, I will keep fighting for it. We must all fight to make sure Americans are never treated in this horrible manner ever again by government bullies.

PART 3

★ ★ ★

Enemies Foreign and Domestic—The TSA and Bullies Abroad

"The right of the people to be secure in their persons, houses, papers, and effects, against unreasonable searches and seizures, shall not be violated..."

—UNITED STATES CONSTITUTION, AMENDMENT IV

13

★ ★ ★

Touching and Squeezing America

"Any society that would give up a little liberty to gain a little security will deserve neither and lose both."

—BENJAMIN FRANKLIN

"If you want total security, go to prison. There you're fed, clothed, given medical care, and so on. The only thing lacking ... is freedom."

—DWIGHT D. EISENHOWER

America's airports have become something between a joke and a nightmare. From infants to grandmothers and everyone in between, no one is spared the routine indignities forced upon travelers by the Transportation Security Administration.

A primary goal of Islamic terrorists, whether on 9/11 or just in general, is to radically change and negatively impact Americans' way of life, to lessen or damage the day-to-day freedoms that Americans have long enjoyed. Terrorists want to make us feel unsafe and scared. They want us to spend America's great wealth chasing them down and occupying countries overseas, to our financial detriment. This is what Islamic extremists did to another global superpower, the Soviet Union, in Afghanistan.

Now they're doing it to us.

The TSA is a grand testament to Islamic terrorists' success—the scene in any airport pre-9/11 verses post-9/11 is now perceived as a major victory by our enemies. We have given up so many of our liberties, all in the name of preventing another tragedy like 9/11—and that's a tragedy in itself.

There are many parts to this tragedy: great expansion of unchecked federal power; agencies first distorting then growing entirely beyond their mission. The combination of all of this has left us where we are today—in a mess. It's funny, I always thought the often uncooperative and time-consuming Department of Motor Vehicles was the worst government department citizens had to deal with on a daily basis—but at least DMV employees stay politely behind the counter and keep their hands to themselves. At the airport, government officials grab our "junk."

In the beginning, it seemed the TSA would simply take over the role of security screening at airports from the private sector, not changing many if any of the standard rules. We were told that these agents would be better trained and better able to treat airport security more like law enforcement. Even the original language used when the TSA was first organized made it sound like it would have more highly trained agents. They weren't even allowed to be unionized, as is much of the federal workforce.

But like most new government programs, the TSA grew and mutated in a very short time.

During my first year in office, public concern over the TSA and its offenses grew stronger. First came the introduction of the "naked body" scanners, which some have accurately dubbed "porno scanners." For years, passengers on airlines, just like visitors to a secure building, have gone through metal detectors to ensure they were not carrying a weapon. In recent years government bureaucrats at the TSA decided that such measures were inadequate. A few isolated and sometimes questionable incidents led to a government and media clamor for even more "security."

Not surprisingly, with each new security "measure" the power of the TSA grew and our individual liberties diminished. Today, our ever-growing national security state shows no signs of slowing.

All of this to keep us "safe." Why? Why don't we take a moment to see how other countries handle airport security.

Israel—perhaps the most secure airline and airport system in the world—has not implemented the use of naked body scanner technology in their airports. Why? Rafi Sela, the thirty-year former head of Israel's airport security, who as part of his tenure helped implement Ben-Gurion International Airport's security, says of these scanners, "You are reacting to incidents instead of being one step ahead of them. I don't know why everybody is running to buy these expensive and useless machines. I can overcome the body scanners with enough explosives to bring down a Boeing 747. That's why we haven't put them in our airport."

That is astounding. The nation most at risk for terrorist attacks—a country considered by nearly everyone to have the best airport security in the world—roundly dismisses the efficiency of the naked body scanner.

So, again, why do we use it? At this point we must revisit a common theme in modern American politics and in this book—the revolving door of politics and business, where the former official becomes able to enrich himself at the taxpayer's expense.

In 2005, the first orders for full body scanners were placed. They were to be part of a test program, commissioned by the Department of Homeland Security and its chief officer, Michael Chertoff.

I am going to give you one guess at what Mr. Chertoff's job became after he left public service.

Chertoff became a lobbyist for the manufacturer of these body scanners, Rapiscan, which at that time was an obscure and fairly small company. But in 2010, after the underwear bomber incident, Chertoff used his credibility as the former head of Homeland Security to make media appearances urging the government to use more naked body scanners. Chertoff became a one-man band in this mission, appearing on talk shows, news programs, radio, print interviews, you name it. You could barely read or watch a report about the failed underwear bomber without also hearing from Michael Chertoff about the need for naked body scanners.

It is hard to blame the media for this. For four years, Chertoff was in charge of Homeland Security. He was an easy and obvious person to reach out to on matters of national security. But did any reporter attempt to investigate exactly what, and who, he was advocating for?

Let's be clear, Michael Chertoff was not acting as a security expert in these interviews. He was acting as a *paid spokesman* for an industry with a huge financial interest in what he was advocating. How much of an interest? It has been estimated that at least one thousand scanners are being used in U.S. airports—at a cost of between $150,000 and $250,000 apiece. Michael Chertoff, former head of Homeland Security and current spokesman for the scanner industry, was advocating for nearly $250 million in sales for his industry.

Is this really how we want our airport security handled? The scanners have a lot of unanswered questions, not the least of which is what level of radiation from these machines is safe. We don't know because this hasn't been studied.

Many Americans were outraged over these new scanners. Whether the argument was safety, privacy, or that they just plain didn't work (they don't), the public outcry was big and loud.

So how did the government address this outcry? They

tried to squash it. Patdowns became even more aggressive—especially for anyone who tried to opt out of going through the scanner. Was the government trying to punish those who opted out? It certainly seemed that way. But these increased and more aggressive patdowns are where the TSA may have made a serious miscalculation concerning what behavior Americans will and will not accept from their government.

Last spring, a six-year-old girl from Bowling Green—a kid from my own backyard—was subjected to a ridiculously invasive search despite her parents' objections. Fortunately for the family, and unfortunately for the TSA, the entire episode was videotaped. It was then shared publicly, embarrassing the TSA—to the degree that this seemingly shameless government agency can even be embarrassed.

I sit on the Senate Homeland Security and Governmental Affairs Committee, which has jurisdiction over part of the TSA. Soon after this incident, the committee held an unrelated hearing with the head of the TSA, John Pistole. I told the story of this six-year-old girl's ordeal with the TSA and asked Mr. Pistole if he could explain the utterly unexplainable event that had just happened to one of my constituents.

Mr. Pistole didn't do himself or his agency much credit that day. He insisted that small children were indeed a risk because a girl in Afghanistan had exploded a bomb in a market. Every single person I talked to after Mr. Pistole's comments, back home or in Washington, D.C., was astounded that his response was to further defend TSA policies.

I could not hold back my disdain for Pistole's analogy. I responded while pointing to the picture of the six-year-old from Kentucky, "You must be clueless if you think this little girl from Bowling Green might be a terrorist!"

I also sent Pistole a written response:

Thank you for your letter of June 30, 2011. I appreciate your inclusion of the materials and your response to our discussion at the recent hearing.

I have to tell you, I was a bit surprised by both the tone and substance of your letter. Your assertions without fact and your wildly unanalogous references to bombings in Afghanistan only reinforce what I thought at our first meeting: The TSA simply does not understand what it should be doing, or how to do it while respecting the rights of law-abiding American citizens.

Equating the groping of a six-year-old girl from Bowling Green, Kentucky, to a jihadist bombing in Afghanistan tells me you either don't understand the problems you are confronting, or simply won't admit the failure of the TSA administrators to write proper rules and procedures.

The logical error here is that you suggest that because a young child in Afghanistan carried a bomb for a terrorist, therefore all American children should be regarded as potential terrorists. Perhaps by searching all American children we are neglecting individuals visiting from countries that have significant jihadist movements.

I will address many of your specific points now.

First, you fail to acknowledge news reports dated June 22 in which a TSA spokesperson was quoted as stating the following: "As part of our ongoing effort to get smarter about security, Administrator Pistole has made a policy decision to give security officers more options for resolving screening anomalies with young children, and we are working to operationalize his decision in airports. This decision will ultimately reduce—though not eliminate—patdowns of children."

This statement was widely described by news reports as a "change" in TSA policy regarding patdowns. Again, however, I see no acknowledgement of any such change in your June 30 letter. You also do not acknowledge concerns expressed by parents around the country who now—as a direct result of TSA's policies—are forced to instruct their children that it is acceptable for government agents to touch them inappropriately.

Second, while I am relieved to hear that TSA is "in discussion" to establish a new "Known" or "Trusted Traveler" program, I remain concerned that—a decade after 9/11—these types of programs are still only at the "discussion" level.

Third, you mention Supreme Court rulings on the right to travel, and you state that you do not believe these rulings apply to travel by aircraft. This precise issue is, of course, a question of law that the U.S. Supreme Court has yet to directly address. However, nothing in the Court's jurisprudence regarding the right to travel supports your argument that government-mandated strip searches are somehow justified because travel by air is only a "privilege."

The right to travel has a firm basis in our nation's history. As far back as the eighteenth century, Sir William Blackstone, the great legal scholar and jurist, declared the following in his *Commentaries on the Laws of England*:

Next to personal security, the law of England regards, asserts, and preserves the personal liberty

of individuals. This personal liberty consists in
the power of loco-motion, of changing situation, or removing one's person to whatsoever
place one's own inclination may direct; without
imprisonment or restraint, unless by due courts
of law.... [Travel] is a right strictly natural...the
laws of England have never abridged it without
sufficient cause...in this kingdom it cannot ever
be abridged at the mere discretion of the magis-
trate, without the explicit permission of the laws.

As you may be aware, Blackstone's *Commentaries*
strongly influenced many of our nation's formative documents, including the Declaration of Independence, the
Constitution, and the Federalist Papers.

In *United States v. Guest*, 383 U.S. 745 (1966), the
U.S. Supreme Court states:

The constitutional right to travel from one State
to another, and necessarily to use the highways
and other instrumentalities of interstate commerce in doing so, occupies a position fundamental to the concept of our Federal Union. It
is a right that has been firmly established and
repeatedly recognized.... [F]reedom to travel
throughout the United States has long been recognized as a basic right under the Constitution.

Id. at 757–58 (internal citations and footnotes omitted).
And in *Saenz v. Roe*, 526 U.S. 489 (1999), the Court
reaffirms this right:

> The word "travel" is not found in the text of the Constitution. Yet the "constitutional right to travel from one State to another" is firmly embedded in our jurisprudence. Indeed, as Justice Stewart reminded us in *Shapiro v. Thompson*, the right is so important that it is "assertable against private interference as well as governmental action,...a virtually unconditional personal right, guaranteed by the Constitution to us all.

Id. at 498 (internal citations omitted).

You argue that travel by aircraft is a "privilege." But this begs the question as to why this so-called "privilege" should be limited to travel by aircraft? If travel by aircraft is a government-bestowed privilege, does it not follow that travel by buses, trains, cars, subways, etc., should also be considered a "privilege"? According to your logic, shouldn't the government be allowed to subject each and every citizen to a strip search prior to entering a bus, train, subway, or even a car, with no probable cause or even reasonable suspicion that a particular individual presents any type of threat? Sidewalks are public property. Does this mean that the TSA should be allowed to set up "strip-search checkpoints" at the end of each sidewalk? While this would arguably make our country a "safer" place, it would also make it a place devoid of liberty, and of all the freedoms which have historically made this country great.

Simply, such logic is the logic of totalitarianism. It is incompatible with our Constitution, which was established to protect citizens from their government, not the government from its citizens.

Finally, I wanted to make sure you saw the enclosed blog post, which presents a question similar to my own inquiry during the hearing. Its author wonders why the TSA regularly stops and subjects young children, the elderly, and the handicapped to "enhanced" patdowns, while a Nigerian man with no ID, carrying expired boarding passes, is somehow able to slip through?

Thank you for your consideration of my concerns.

But no one should have been astounded. Government agencies will never do anything on their own to alter or correct absurd policies. Only the political reality of a public backlash could force them to change. One way to change these draconian TSA policies is for people to tell their stories. One story is bad news for the TSA. A dozen is worse. A hundred becomes a problem.

A thousand becomes an outcry.

I want to share some TSA horror stories, but, in telling them, also urge action. Stand up for your rights. Do this every day. Don't let mere convenience silence you. Always be polite, but firm, in knowing what your government can and cannot make you do.

Going through security at the airport in Nashville in January 2012, I was detained for not agreeing to a patdown after an irregularity was found in my full-body scan. I refused the patdown.

I showed the agents the potentially dangerous part of my body—my leg. They were not interested. These agents insisted they must touch me and pat me down. I requested to be rescanned. They refused and detained me in a ten-foot-square area reserved for potential terrorists.

Let me be clear: I neither asked for nor expected any special treatment for being a U.S. senator. But my experience wasn't really about me at all. It was about every single one of us. It was about how we are sick of our increasingly arrogant and intrusive government.

Sitting in the cubicle, I thought to myself, "Have the terrorists won?" Have we—as Benjamin Franklin once famously warned we should never do—sacrificed our liberty and our basic dignity for security?

Passengers who do everything right—remove their belts, their wallets, their shoes, their glasses, and all of the contents in their pockets—are then subjected to random patdowns and tricked into believing that the scanners actually do something.

Random screenings not based on risk assessments misdirect the screening process. They also grossly and unnecessarily add to the already existing indignity of travel. Those passengers who suffer through the process of partially disrobing should at the very least be rewarded with less invasive examination.

This agency's disregard for our civil liberties is something we are expected to understand and accept. Americans increasingly neither understand it not accept it.

The TSA was created in the aftermath of the September 11 terrorist attacks, but was it necessary? Has it overstepped its bounds? Is it respecting the rights of citizens?

I certainly didn't feel like my rights were respected when I was detained and harassed by the TSA. I've since heard from countless Americans who feel the same way. They, too, feel their liberties are being compromised every time they travel. My office is constantly inundated with countless stories of assault and harassment by the TSA.

It is time for us to question the effectiveness of our methods. It is time for us to reexamine how much of our liberty we have traded for security.

America can prosper, preserve personal liberty, and repel national security threats without intruding into the personal lives of its citizens. Every time we travel, we are expected to surrender our Fourth Amendment rights. Yet willingly giving up our rights does not make us any safer. It is infuriating that this agency feels entitled to revoke our civil liberties while doing little to keep us safe.

Is the TSA looking at flight manifests? Are we researching those boarding the planes? Are we targeting or looking at those who might more potentially attack us? Apparently not. The TSA instead wastes its time patting down six-year-old girls.

This blatant violation of the Fourth Amendment, which protects Americans against unwarranted search and seizure, has insulted many citizens, and rightfully so. I, along with many other travelers, do not view traveling as a crime that warrants government search and seizure. In fact, I view traveling as a basic right, in which Americans should be free to travel from state to state as they please.

It is my firm belief that TSA should not have such broad authority to violate our constitutional rights with these ineffective and invasive physical searches. In my fight for these basic rights, I will further push for the reinstatement of traveler privacy and rights. I will be proposing two pieces of legislation: first, the Air Travelers' Bill of Rights, which will be explained further in a later chapter, and second—and this is the ultimate goal—the privatization of the TSA.

It is much easier to take away citizens' freedom while wearing a government badge. It is just a fact.

Many airports, including recently one of the busiest in the world in Orlando, have petitioned the federal government to get the TSA removed from their airports. Why? Because that is what the airports are hearing from their customers. Air travel, like most other things in our country, would be safer, cheaper, and more tolerable if the government and their armed bullies got out of the way.

So we have the bullies. We have the Beseechers. We have corruption and greed mixed with the natural desire of government to make us feel safer and more secure at all costs, even if the methods don't work.

That's the TSA. Let us now examine, in real, flesh-and-blood terms, the kind of outrageous behavior this out-of-control government agency regularly visits upon everyday Americans.

14

★ ★ ★

How the TSA Terrorizes
American Citizens

"The next time airport security tells you to put your hands over your head and hold that vulnerable position for seven seconds, ask yourself: Is this the posture of a free man?"

—NOAH FELDMAN, HARVARD LAW PROFESSOR

Since my ordeal with the TSA made national headlines, the phones in my office have been ringing off of the hook with calls from citizens who sympathize with my frustration. Many Americans feel their liberties are being compromised every time they travel. My office has been inundated with stories of assault, harassment, theft, and bullying at the hands of TSA agents. The agency's utter disregard for our civil liberties is something we are supposed to simply expect, understand, and accept. But we are Americans. We are not supposed to be treated like this by government officials. We are tired of being insulted. We are tired of having our dignity compromised. It is fundamentally wrong that any government can force its citizens to consent to invasive searches anytime we want to travel. The Fourth Amendment is not simply some trivial piece of legislation to be ignored at government whim, but an integral part of all Americans' constitutional liberties.

These personal stories of physical and mental abuse by the TSA involve groping, bullying, harassment, theft, or even a combination of all four. Some of the stories include shocking privacy violations and literal molestation.

In 2010, the TSA implemented new screening measures that further increased the invasive nature of the agency. One of these new measures required TSA agents to literally put their hands down people's pants if they were wearing baggy clothing. Since this procedure was implemented, there have been thousands of reports of sexual molestation and related violations. New Jersey–based radio host Owen JJ Stone, known as "OhDoctah" to his fans, shared his horrific TSA screening experience with his listeners.

While traveling, Stone was motioned to approach TSA agents, who told him that because he was wearing sweatpants, he must undergo a patdown. When he asked what this patdown would entail, the TSA agent said, "I have to go in your waistband and I have to put my hands down your pants." The agent offered to perform this in a private room. Understandably apprehensive about what was about to happen, Stone instead chose to have the search conducted in public view, fearful that the agent would be more aggressive and invasive in private. Stone described in stark terms what happened next— the agent put his hands inside Stone's pants and directly patted down his testicles, penis, and backside.

An ABC News producer had a similar experience involving TSA molestation. She chose to opt out of a full-body scan, so the TSA required her to stand aside and receive a patdown. She explained, "The woman who checked me reached her hands inside my underwear and felt her way around. It was basically worse than going to the gynecologist." These invasive searches do not ensure our safety, but they do ensure molestation and embarrassment. Understandably, the producer said she found the entire process embarrassing, demeaning, and inappropriate.

Many female travelers have been sexually victimized by this government agency. Eliana S. went through security at the

Orlando International Airport, where she felt personally victimized by the male TSA agents. She felt objectified as two male TSA agents stared at her as she waited in the security line. They were pointing, whispering, and blatantly eyeballing her, looking her body up and down. These agents asked her to step aside after she walked through the scanner, informing her that they had to perform a patdown. She said it was very uncomfortable and she felt sexually violated.

Actress and former *Baywatch* star Donna D'Errico had a similar experience while traveling. A male TSA agent told her she had been singled out for a patdown. When she asked why, the agent replied, "You caught my eye, and they [other travelers] didn't." While she was being patted down, other agents gathered around to watch. She felt objectified and violated by government officials and there was absolutely nothing she could do about it. D'Errico said, "The TSA decides for you that you will consent to being scanned or felt up, or you simply won't be allowed your constitutional right to travel."

Former Miss USA Susie Castillo always opts out of the full-body scanner. She believes it is harmful to her health. So instead, she is routinely forced to undergo patdowns conducted by TSA agents. During one particular instance, Castillo said that the TSA agent "actually felt and touched my vagina." Outraged, Castillo used social media to spread awareness of the TSA's frequent sexual molestation and rampant abuse of the Fourth Amendment.

The TSA's invasive procedures are not always sexual, but they are most certainly always embarrassing. Thomas Sawyer, sixty-one, fell victim to the agency's embarrassing and degrading practices while traveling out of the Detroit

Metropolitan Airport. Sawyer is a bladder cancer survivor. Due to his health condition, he is forced to carry a urostomy bag. During a patdown, a TSA agent broke the seal of his bag, drenching Sawyer in urine.

An elderly and ill citizen was humiliated by the TSA in northwest Florida. The ninety-five-year-old leukemia patient was traveling with her daughter when she was forced to partake in a random patdown. The agents claimed they found something suspicious around the woman's leg and took her into a private room. While performing the screening in the private room, agents claimed they couldn't perform a thorough search because her Depends underwear were "wet and firm." The woman was forced to take off her undergarments, finish the screening process, and then walk through the airport without any underwear.

Tammy B., fifty-two, was also publicly humiliated by the TSA while being screened. Tammy is wheelchair-bound and had often had problems with security during travel. After an uncomfortable and invasive search two weeks prior, she wore simply a trench coat and undergarments as a means of avoiding any more invasive searches. Tammy was literally stripped down to her undergarments, while the TSA publicly searched her. This "routine" search lasted over an hour and left her in nothing but her underwear for all passersby to see.

Mandi H., thirty-seven, was also publicly humiliated by TSA. While traveling out of the Lubbock airport in Texas, Mandi set off the metal detector with her nipple piercings. She explained this to the TSA agents, and they asked her to remove the piercings. Crying from humiliation, Mandi told agents that she could not remove them without pliers. Skin typically heals around the piercing and removing them is incredibly painful. The agents quickly supplied her with pliers, and as she removed her body jewelry, several agents looked on, snickering and whispering. She felt publicly objectified and humiliated for wearing personal jewelry. The last time I checked, body jewelry was not a dangerous weapon, nor is it a threat to the safety and security of the United States.

Apparently, the TSA publicly humiliates new mothers as well. Amy S., a nursing mother, was boarding a plane in Hawaii with her newborn baby girl, Eva. As if traveling with a newborn isn't hassle enough, the TSA was determined to make her journey even more difficult. The agents told her that she was not allowed to board the plane with her breast pump unless she pumped milk into empty bottles, to prove that the device was in fact a breast pump. Amy explained, "I asked if there was a private place I could pump and he said, no, you can go in the women's restroom." The only electrical outlet in the restroom was next to a sink, surrounded by a wall of mirrors. "I had to stand in front of the mirrors and the sinks to pump my breasts, in front of every tourist that walked into that bathroom," she said. She said that the entire experience left her feeling embarrassed and humiliated. The TSA publicly humiliates travelers in this manner on a regular basis, while doing very little to actually keep us safe.

Children also fall victim to the TSA's abuse. Four-year-old Ryan T. was born sixteen weeks premature. Developmentally disabled, he has to wear leg braces because his ankles are malformed and his legs are not fully developed. This young boy only recently learned to walk on his own, and can only take a few small steps before needing support. In March 2009, his parents took him to Disney World. If any child deserved a vacation and some fun, it was Ryan. But while traveling through security at the Philadelphia airport, his family ran into some problems. The TSA did not care that Ryan was a four-year-old child with disabilities. They did not care that he relied on his leg braces for support. As his mother carried him through the scanner, the alarm went off, as expected. The agent replied that Ryan must take off his braces and walk through the scanner on his own. The mother attempted to explain that Ryan could barely walk with his braces, let alone without them. The compassionless screener did not care. Exhausted from arguing with these bullying screeners, Ryan's parents finally succumbed to their demands. According to senior TSA authorities, Ryan should never have been forced to remove his braces. But the senior authorities' response was too late. The agency expressed a "better luck next time" reaction to the whole ordeal. The TSA has yet to issue a formal apology to the Thomas family.

An eight-month-old baby was frisked by TSA screeners while traveling out of Kansas City International Airport. The baby's stroller set off an alarm in the scanner, so of course TSA agents felt they just had to pat down an eight-month-old baby. *An eight-month-old child!* This is extreme abuse by our government and certainly has nothing to do with our safety. It is an infringement of our constitutional rights. Our government is harming citizens, not helping them.

When I read that eight-month-old children are being frisked before they fly, I can't help but think that the terrorists have won. They have so changed our day-to-day way of life that we voluntarily give up our constitutional right to simply fly from one state to another.

If the TSA isn't sexually harassing you, invading your personal space, or humiliating you, chances are they might be stealing from you. Since 2007 over three dozen TSA agents have been fired for stealing from checked and unchecked baggage. In 2009, a former TSA agent at Newark Liberty Airport was charged with stealing between $200,000 and $400,000 worth of electronics, jewelry, and money from passengers in transit. In the same New Jersey airport, two agents were charged with three counts of theft, one count of conspiring to commit theft, and one count of accepting bribes. These agents targeted foreign passengers flying via Air India. They would steal money from the passengers' luggage or small carry-on items while they went through the screening area. On average, the agents would steal approximately $400–$700 per shift. One TSA agent was accused of stealing money from a passenger in 2010. While searching a passenger's purse, he pocketed almost $500 of the woman's money. The passenger immediately noticed that the money was missing and complained to supervisors. Security cameras showed the agent taking the money out of the woman's purse and putting it in his back pocket.

When traveling, we are not only expected to hand over our purses, laptop cases, briefcases, backpacks, and duffel bags— we are also expected to hand over our dignity and constitutional rights. Just trying to take a vacation, we are expected to surrender our Fourth Amendment rights. Surrendering these rights and our civil liberties has done little to actually keep us safe.

The TSA should not be at liberty to universally insult all travelers—they should, however, research, track, monitor, and target people who are in fact actual threats to our nation.

The TSA's primary function as an agency is to blatantly violate the Fourth Amendment, which protects Americans against unwarranted search and seizure. This agency has insulted and humiliated countless American citizens. I, along with many other travelers, do not view traveling as a crime that warrants routine government-enforced search and seizure. In fact, I view traveling as a basic right, in which Americans should be free to travel from one state to another without having to succumb to sexual harassment, public humiliation, and government theft—of both our possessions and our pride.

America is better than this.

15

★ ★ ★

How Can We Solve the Problem?

"'Security theater' refers to security measures that make people feel more secure without doing anything to actually improve their security."
—BRUCE SCHNEIER, SECURITY SPECIALIST

"If tyranny and oppression come to this land it will be in the guise of fighting a foreign enemy."
—JAMES MADISON

The right to travel "is a right broadly assertable against private interference as well as governmental action. Like the right of association...it is a virtually unconditional personal right, guaranteed by the Constitution to us all" (Supreme Court justice Potter Stewart, *Shapiro v. Thompson*, 1969).

You've heard my personal story concerning the TSA. You've read much worse stories in this book. You can find a dozen more similar stories on any given day, simply by reading or watching the news. The regular abuse of the American people by our increasingly police-state government—the TSA being a prime example—cannot be overestimated or denied.

I sympathize with the problems political leaders have had to deal with in this post–9/11 era. But legislators and executives have had to contend with such problems for as long as there have been governments.

When something bad happens, to whatever degree, there is always someone clamoring for the government to "DO SOMETHING!" about it. Understandably, such outcries often come from the victims or their families. But more often the cry for government "solutions" comes from journalists, eager to stoke the fire.

Such is the nature of the irrevocably intertwined worlds of politics and journalism. Consider the following, not so uncommon scenario: A young reporter and a young city councilman each begin their respective careers. The councilman needs to get his message out; the reporter needs a message to cover. They work in conjunction as a matter of circumstance.

A tragedy happens in their hometown. A somewhat busy street corner with no traffic light becomes the site of an accident, causing the death of young students on their way home from school. It is a horrible tragedy. We've all seen stories like this, and our hearts always go out to the victims and their families in any tragedy.

The journalist interviews local citizens who say they want a traffic light at that corner. If only a traffic light had been there, they say, the accident could have been avoided. Never mind that the other car was speeding, the driver was drunk, and a traffic light probably wouldn't have stopped him anyway—such logic or facts are beside the point.

The journalist writes story after story about this issue. People start showing up at city council meetings. Groups are organized. Flyers are distributed. The public wants a traffic light, and with it, hopefully a better sense of security.

The politician sees an opportunity. He can instantly be a hero to his constituents. So of course he fights for and ultimately gets the traffic light.

This is a small example, but the lesson remains the same— government grows. The government solution itself would have done little to nothing to prevent the tragedy the traffic light was meant to address. It does little to prevent possible future tragedies. Still, the journalist wins a prize for his coverage of the event. The politician ends up getting elected mayor. The guy who owns the traffic light company makes a profit.

Such scenarios are repeated day after day, in city after city across the United States, and this has been the case for a very long time. But while a traffic light is no big deal, here's where it gets more troubling. Imagine that the local journalist has worked his way up to the *New York Times.* The former councilman turned mayor has become a U.S. senator. Larger tragedies strike. Greater government action is clamored for. Perhaps even some corporations stand to make significant profits through these "solutions."

The players involved, from the reporter to the politician, grew up in and around politics. This is all they know. They believe that every tragedy, no matter how it occurred, whether great or small, must be followed by journalists and politicians rushing to "do something."

Many of the government reactions to 9/11 were justified. Many of them were not, and those experiences should teach some lessons. But let's first talk about a few things we did that made sense.

In 2001, we had in our possession a prisoner with a laptop. On that laptop were many of the details of the 9/11 plot. But we didn't find this out until much later.

Why? When this man was first arrested, we found nothing. The bureaucracies supposedly responsible for handling such matters were not functioning properly, if at all. Local field agents in Minnesota, where the prisoner and laptop were captured, requested dozens of times from their superiors permission to seek a warrant to enable them to investigate further, including looking at the suspect's laptop. But nothing was done.

The man in custody was Zacarias Moussaoui, often referred to as the twentieth hijacker. He had direct links to eleven of the nineteen hijackers. He had travel and financial information about the 9/11 attacks. There was clear-cut evidence of this man's guilt and complicity in carrying out the attacks.

But we didn't know it.

Remarkably, no one at the FBI was fired over this, then or to this day. No one was held responsible. This has always galled me—that even though three thousand innocent people lost their lives and gross incompetence was shown throughout the investigation, no one had to pay the price. No one lost their job.

No, instead, several agents received medals and commendations. Our government reacted by creating an even *bigger* bureaucracy—the Department of Homeland Security.

What we should have done was to consolidate agencies, tearing down the red tape and bureaucratic walls that prevent the sharing of information, being effective, and simply communicating with each other, and make our entire law enforcement and intelligence culture more accountable in achieving results.

But there were good reactions: We took steps to put air marshals on planes. Pilots are now allowed to arm themselves. We have reinforced, locked cockpit doors and we have much more training and awareness among flight crews about how to safeguard the airplane, the lives of the passengers, and potential victims on the ground.

But the most helpful reaction to terrorists wanting to use a plane as a weapon didn't come after 9/11 through government action. It came *on* 9/11—through the example of the heroes on United Flight 93.

Those brave passengers on board that day had heard of what had just happened to the World Trade Center. They knew this was not a typical hijacking, where the plane would simply land somewhere and the hijackers would make demands. Those passengers knew that thousands or perhaps tens of thousands of innocent people might die if the hijackers succeeded in crashing the plane.

So they acted. They overpowered the hijackers and took down the plane themselves, sacrificing their lives to save countless others. No one knows for sure how many lives they saved that day. It is hard to imagine an act of heroism any greater.

That reaction, by those passengers on that dark day, makes it highly unlikely that terrorists will ever be able to use a plane as a weapon as they did on 9/11. The passengers simply will not allow it. The passengers of Flight 93 did more that day to stop another 9/11 than our government has done in the eleven years since.

Still, this doesn't stop the government from "trying."

The federal government's reaction was to create the dog-and-pony show that is the Transportation Security Administration. We've seen the problems and read the stories. So what's the solution?

The solution is to take a step back. We are not preventing another 9/11 through this massive government boondoggle. The TSA is more security "theater" than security reality. We are not safer, we are just less free.

I have a two-pronged solution for the TSA.

I don't actually want two solutions. My first solution is my favorite. It is the simplest and most positive thing we can do: End the TSA as we know it.

My bill would privatize all screeners, as they had previously been. The person at that checkpoint should not have the power of a government badge on their side. They should simply be the conduit in a private transaction—you, the private citizen, have contracted with the airline, a private company, to provide transportation. All the government does is muck it up.

If the security is in the hands of the airlines and airports, they have to still treat you as customers. As a matter of good business, they will have to treat you with respect. They have to design rules that both move their commerce along and keep it safe.

Airlines and airports have a great interest in their product being safe. It would put them out of business quickly if there were a rash of attacks. They too would've had reactions and solutions after 9/11, but government stepped in before we had a chance to see what those solutions would've been.

Unlike private entities, government has no incentive to make its product customer-friendly—or even human-friendly, in my experience. It's like going to the Department of Motor Vehicles, but somehow it takes even longer and involves groping you. (I sincerely hope no one at the DMV is reading this and thinking of adding groping to that experience as well.)

So my bill forces the government to get out of the airline business—to get out of our business. Let the airlines and the airports hire the contractors and largely put the systems in place, leaving in place some minimum government rules and oversight. This is by far the easiest and best solution.

But since I know government often has no interest in the easiest or best solution, I have also introduced what I call the Air Travelers' Bill of Rights. These are rules that the TSA must follow for as long as they are still in charge of security at the airports.

Many of the TSA's screening procedures simply defy common sense, such as "enhanced patdowns" of elderly passengers, young children, or those with disabilities. It seems that every day we hear a new story about mistreatment at the hands of TSA agents during the screening process. While aviation security is undoubtedly important, we must be diligent in protecting Americans from being subjected to humiliating and intrusive searches by TSA agents, especially when there is no obvious cause.

It is important that the rules and boundaries of our airport screening process be transparent and easily available to travelers so that proper restraints are in place on screeners. Travelers should be empowered with the knowledge necessary to protect themselves from a violation of their rights and dignity.

Among the seventeen minimum rights laid out in the Air Travelers' Bill of Rights:

- A TSA screener "opt-out" for airports, allowing them access to the Screening Partnership Program (SPP) and private screeners;
- A one-year deadline to implement a screening process for precleared frequent fliers at all airports with more than 250,000 annual flights;
- Authority to permit travelers who fail to pass imaging or metal detector screening to choose to be rescreened rather than subjected to an automatic patdown;
- Expansion of canine screening at airports, a more effective and less invasive method of screening passengers for explosives, as well as a strong deterrent;
- Eliminating unnecessary patdowns for children twelve years of age or under;

- Right of parents to stay with their children during the screening process;
- Guaranteeing a traveler's right to request a patdown using only the back of the hand;
- Protection of a traveler's right to appropriately object to mistreatment by screeners;
- Protection of a traveler's right to decline a backscatter X-ray scan, a screening method with potentially harmful health effects;
- Protection of a traveler's right to contact an attorney if detained or removed from screening.

The bill would require these and other reforms be collected into a single "bill of rights" to be distributed by the TSA at all airports and featured on the TSA's website. This bill of rights would remain in force whether or not the TSA or the airlines ran the screening.

Our current approach—that everyone is an equal risk of being a terrorist—makes us less safe. By wasting time patting down six-year-olds we are spending less time monitoring the guy who has been to Yemen three times in the last year. Instead of harassing Grandma, I'd rather know where each of the eighty thousand students visiting from the Middle East are. I want to know when students visiting from Pakistan or Saudi Arabia are getting on a train, plane, or bus, and am much less concerned with where the salesman from Omaha travels every week.

Wouldn't it be nice to look forward to getting on a plane again? I remember as a younger man being very interested in flight. It is a magical and wonderful thing we have invented, to take us across the heavens to visit our loved ones or enjoy a much-needed vacation.

We can be safe while being free. Not 100 percent safe—but then no measure of security can make us 100 percent safe, and anyone who tells you that it can is lying to you.

Or perhaps selling the "security" equipment.

16

Foreign Bullies

"Whatever crushes individuality is despotism."
—John Stuart Mill

* * *

In the spring of 2012, I met in my Senate conference room with David Kramer, president of the human rights advocacy organization Freedom House. We were joined by his staff and Nancy Okail, an Egyptian mother, wife, and political activist who had an important life decision to make—a decision that included not only her, but her husband and children. She was visibly upset throughout the meeting. She feared for her family's safety. She feared for her own safety.

Mrs. Okail had been the victim of her own government. She was separated from her husband and children. She was taken from her family and threatened with jail. She was hauled before a kangaroo court and put in a cage in front of the judge. She was humiliated by a prosecutor. She was threatened with five years of hard time in an Egyptian prison, not generally regarded as a safe place for a young and attractive woman. She was unsure whether to return to Egypt and face her harsh prison sentence or stay in the United States.

Okail was one of the international democracy workers who had been detained in Egypt in late December 2011 by that nation's military dictatorship. The charges were completely fabricated. She had done nothing wrong, nor had the nineteen Americans who had also been held.

Thankfully, I helped secure these innocent people's freedom in a battle that went from the cloakroom of the Senate to
the halls of power in Cairo. Allow me to explain.

In December 2011, Egyptian and foreign activists (including the nineteen U.S. citizens) were detained by the Egyptian
government. They were charged with running an "unregistered NGO" (nongovernmental organization) that had allegedly received foreign funding for their activities.

For years, groups like Freedom House, the International
Republican Institute, and the National Democratic Institute
have used a combination of private funds and State Department funding to help promote democracy and civil society
abroad. This has been an ongoing effort since the Reagan
administration, and these groups' activities have always had
broad bipartisan and international support.

These organizations are not partisan. They do not choose
political sides. They do not provoke or become involved in the
politics of any country they work in. They do not encourage or
cause dissent. They do not advocate against government.

When Egyptian president Hosni Mubarak was ousted from
office in 2011, various Egyptian factions struggled to assem-
ble and consolidate power, from the military to the Muslim
Brotherhood and leftovers from the Mubarak regime.

It was a member of Mubarak's old guard who decided to
charge these agencies and their workers with the "crime" of
doing something they had been doing legally and with full
permission for years.

American and Egyptian citizens were arrested. Obviously
my first concern was the detained Americans, whose plight
I immediately trumpeted. After later hearing how the Egyptians were treated, I wish I had fought harder for all involved.

One of the Americans arrested was Sam LaHood, the son of Obama's secretary of transportation, Ray LaHood. No doubt this helped the story gain initial traction and attention. I spoke to my colleagues about this issue, particularly those with plenty of experience in foreign affairs, in an attempt to see how to best address the detainment of the Americans.

I waited patiently, while I was also being told that we had to be careful. I was told that the situation in Egypt was volatile and that we had to make sure whatever we did actually helped the situation.

While I understood this, I also couldn't help but feel that there was an alarming lack of action. I felt like some involved were more interested in protecting their political turf than in protecting American citizens.

I do not have forty years of foreign policy experience. But I do know that if you want a take on a bully, you can't be meek. You don't pull punches, but swing as hard as you can, preferably with a blunt object.

My blunt object was foreign aid. Due to a near criminal degree of corruption, abuse, and waste on the part of many recipients—not to mention the fact that we can't afford it—I had long been in favor of eliminating foreign aid altogether. But since the aid existed, I thought it gave Congress the perfect tool to help the detained Americans.

I looked for an opportunity on the Senate floor to take action. There was no obvious vehicle. Therefore I did what any good, sensible, and responsible senator would do—I attempted to attach an amendment to freeze aid to Egypt to the Postal Reform Act. Some of my colleagues were confused. Some were amused. Others were angry. It just depended on who you spoke to.

Once on the floor, I offered to simply hold a vote on my amendment with only ten minutes of discussion. I was honestly trying to make it easier on Majority Leader Harry Reid. I knew he didn't want to discuss this and would likely claim lack of time as the reason.

So I offered to vote immediately at any time—and made the point that it was well worth ten minutes of the Senate's time to discuss the plight of U.S. citizens being held illegally in Egypt. Indeed, what American would find ten minutes of discussion too much to ask concerning whether or not Egypt should receive U.S. aid while also detaining our citizens? We had sent Mubarak's regime over $60 billion and now a member of that same regime was responsible for arresting and holding American citizens against their will—nineteen U.S. nationals who had traveled to Egypt to help that country embrace democracy, to have an elected government so that Egyptians might enjoy the same kind of freedoms we do.

Some of the Americans arrested sought refuge in the U.S. embassy. This was tragic. This was something the United States should make a clear and unequivocal statement about. Did Egypt wish to be part of the civilized world or did it want to continue to descend into third-world lawlessness?

I proposed an amendment to end *all* foreign aid to Egypt—economic aid, military aid, all aid—in thirty days unless the American citizens were released. We give over $1.5 billion to Egypt annually. Fiscally, we can't afford this. Morally, with Egypt detaining our own people, we couldn't afford this.

If Egypt or any other country wanted to act against the interests of the United States, particularly harming our citizens abroad, they needed to know that America does not tolerate it. Such countries needed to know that we mean business.

That's what this debate was about.

We have sent billions of dollars to Africa to authoritarian regimes that rape, pillage, and torture their own people. We continue to give them more money each year in the hope that they might one day change their ways. It hasn't worked.

We need a firmer hand. We need a stronger voice. We need to say no more aid to countries that do not have democratic elections, no more aid to nations that terrorize their own people—*and no more aid to anyone who detains innocent American citizens!*

We continue sending billions to Afghanistan, yet Afghan president Hamid Karzai says that if neighboring Pakistan and the United States went to war, his country would side with Pakistan. Why exactly are we sending so much money to Afghanistan?

Pakistani leaders have made similar comments, that if the United States goes to war with Iran, Pakistan will side with Iran. Yet we continue to send Pakistan billions of U.S. taxpayer dollars. Why?

We cannot continue to try to buy allies or pay off our enemies. So many of the countries we send aid to dislike us, regularly disrespect us, and openly tell the world they will side with our enemies.

America doesn't even have the money to send them. We're borrowing the money from China to aid people who don't like us. This is illogical. It's an insult.

And it should end.

Egypt had to be put on notice. The president and the State Department were not making any substantive attempts to lead on this issue. Just a few weeks prior, the president's undersecretary of state Robert Hormats stated publicly that the Obama administration wanted to assure the Egyptians that the United States intended to provide continuing aid and benefits.

Do you think that was the right message to send Egypt? That although Egypt was detaining nineteen U.S. citizens, preventing them from leaving, preventing them from coming home—that the Egyptian government could be assured that U.S. aid would continue?

American citizens were essentially trapped in our embassy in Egypt and the Obama administration was assuring the Egyptians that they would receive their benefits immediately.

The day before my floor speech about my amendment, the president introduced his new budget. Guess what it included? One and a half billion taxpayer dollars for Egypt.

What kind of message are we sending the world?

President Obama was not leading the country. He was not exemplifying what most Americans would obviously want—to send a clear and unequivocal message to Egypt that we would not tolerate this behavior, certainly that we would not subsidize this behavior.

Yet we did. We do. American taxpayers subsidize a government that detains innocent U.S. citizens. American taxpayers subsidize Afghanistan, a nation that would side with Pakistan over the United States. American taxpayers subsidize Pakistan, a nation that would side with Iran over the United States.

We do this as we bankrupt our own country by running up trillion-dollar deficits with borrowed money.

The Senate unquestionably needed to discuss this. The country needed to discuss this. Fortunately, I was in a position to do something about it.

My efforts were certainly worth it for the nineteen detained U.S. citizens. If it were my child in Egypt, working there for a pro-democracy group, I would want to think that the U.S. Senate had at least ten minutes to devote to discussing my child's fate abroad. I would want to think that the Senate could also spare ten minutes to send the Egyptians an unequivocal statement: The United States will not stand for the detention of its citizens, their imprisonment, or unreasonable travel restrictions. The United States will not send aid to a government that so casually abuses our own people.

I knew some would say that I was holding up the business of the Senate—but I was saying that *this should be the business of the Senate!* The Constitution grants these types of foreign policy decisions to Congress, and that we would ignore this particular case was an ominous reminder of just how much we have abdicated our proper constitutional role.

When I gave my floor speech, instead of agreeing to the ten minutes of debate and taking a vote on my amendment, the Senate literally shut down. Majority Leader Reid simply refused to allow the Senate to even consider the issue, while simultaneously accusing me of all sorts of horrors. His absurd and disjointed accusations had something to do with old liberal bugaboos about Republicans like me hating old people and the poor. Reid simply didn't make any sense.

After the Senate shutdown, I had several discussions with prominent senators who took an interest in this area of the world. While they had publicly said that perhaps I was being rash, and that perhaps we should hold off on trying to stop foreign aid, privately these senators were telling me a different story. They were telling me that while they disagreed with ending aid, they lauded my tactic of putting pressure on Esypt. They told me they were happy I was willing to take this particular stand.

At the end of that week, several of those senators left Washington for Egypt in order to attend previously scheduled private meetings with Egyptian leaders that weekend. After these meetings, these senators told me that my amendment was a topic of discussion, and that the Egyptians had become very concerned about keeping their foreign aid. The senators, in a bit of international "good cop/bad cop," explained to the Egyptians that they had held me off for now, but when they returned it was unlikely they could continue to stop my amendment from coming up to a vote. They told the Egyptians that if my amendment did come up for a vote before the Senate, it might just pass.

It certainly would be a tough vote. What senator would want to publicly vote to give foreign aid to a country that was holding American citizens against their will?

After the Senate recessed on the day my amendment was prevented from being voted on, I took to the floor to chastise the Senate leadership and my colleagues. Here is an excerpt from my remarks:

> Dependency often leads to indolence, lethargy, and a sense of entitlement and ultimately to a state of insolence.
>
> Egypt has been receiving welfare from the United States for nearly forty years now. America has lavished over $60 billion on the government of Egypt, and they react with insolence and disregard by detaining nineteen of our U.S. citizens.
>
> For several months now, these Americans have been essentially held hostage, unable to leave Egypt, held on the pretense of trumped-up political charges, held in order to display them in show trials to placate the mob.

The United States can respond in one of two ways. We can hang our head low and take the tack of Jimmy Carter. We could try to placate Egypt with concessions and offer them bribes in the form of more government aid.

Or America could respond with strength.

The president should today call the Egyptian ambassador in and send him home with a message—a message that America will not tolerate any country holding U.S. citizens as political prisoners.

Congress should act today to tell Egypt that we will no longer send our annual welfare check to them; that this year's $1.8 billion is not on the way.

America could put Egyptian travelers on notice that the welcome sign in America will temporarily expire unless the Egyptian government lets our people go. Or America could hang her head low, promise to continue foreign aid to Egypt, and apologize for supporting democracy. Which will it be?

So far, the signals sent to Egypt from the president and from the Senate have been weak or counterproductive.

In late January, the president's undersecretary of state said that the administration wants to provide "more immediate benefits" to Egypt. Let's speed up the welfare checks. The president's budget this week includes the $1.8 billion for Egypt without a word of rebuke or any demand for our citizens to be released.

The president went one step further. He actually increased the foreign aid to the Middle East in his budget. And now the Senate refuses to even hold a single vote to spend ten minutes discussing why U.S. citizens are being detained in Egypt.

One might excuse the Egyptians for not believing we will cut their aid. You can't lead from behind.

Senate leadership appears unwilling to address this issue head-on. So the Senate won't act to help our citizens this week. But I hope when senators return home this week to their constituents in their state, I hope their constituents will ask them these questions:

Senator, why do you continue to send our taxpayer money to Egypt? Why do you continue to send our money to Egypt when they detain U.S. citizens?

Senator, why do you continue to send billions of dollars to Egypt when twelve million Americans are out of work?

Senator, why do you continue to send welfare to foreign countries, when our bridges are falling down and in desperate need of repair?

Senator, how can you continue to flush our taxpayer money down a foreign drain, when we are borrowing $40,000 a second? The money we send to Egypt we must first borrow from China. That is insanity and it must end.

Mr. Senator, I hope your constituents ask you this when you go home: When working families are suffering under rising food prices, when working families are suffering because gas prices have doubled, how can you justify sending our hard-earned taxpayer dollars to Egypt? To countries that openly show their disdain for us?

There were national news stories about this issue, and I returned to Washington the following week more determined than ever to get the detained Americans out of danger and end this crisis.

I made sure to let the leadership of both parties know that there was no backing down. They would not move anything through the Senate without my consent until this mess was straightened out.

The senators who had been to Egypt returned and told me of their conversations with that country's leaders, who not only wanted the aid, but also seemed to want the NGOs to return to operation as they had done for years.

On that Monday, Senator Reid announced that my amendment would in fact get a vote that week in order to move Senate business forward.

Word apparently traveled fast to Cairo. Reading the political winds and heeding the warnings of the Senate delegation, the Egyptian government announced the release of the American detainees the next day.

While there are obviously many things going on at once in a situation like this—many moving parts, many players—I was glad that I could help, in my capacity as a U.S. senator, those who needed it.

But some battles can't be won simply from our Senate offices. Those that call for pushback against a government, whether ours, abroad, or both, often require pressure that must be applied before the public. I can inform the public— and an informed public can help apply the political pressure necessary to overcome the inherent inertia of Congress.

Making battles public gives us all greater influence. When the grassroots loudly engages, it can even trump seniority on the Hill. Nothing pleases me more than to give voice to millions of Americans who rightly want me to champion certain causes— from ridiculous light bulb bans to illegally detained Americans— that ordinary Americans would if they were in my position.

Sometimes this baffles my colleagues, and understandably so. Though I like and admire many of my colleagues, they are not ordinary Americans.

Concerning the Americans detained in Egypt, ordinary Americans—through me—were able to vent their frustration over an indefensible situation. And indefensible situations that are exposed to public scrutiny have a much better chance of getting fixed.

On March 1, 2012, the problem was at least temporarily solved: The Egyptian government announced that the detained Americans were free to leave Egypt.

I say it was "temporarily" solved because it later came to light that our State Department had in fact paid "bail" (more like a ransom) for our citizens' release, and that they had all agreed to return to Egypt should there be a trial, an agreement I am sure few, if any, intended to keep.

So was this issue really solved?

My focus, as I noted earlier, was wholly on the release of the Americans. But as I mentioned earlier, the threat did not begin, nor did it end, with the American citizens.

Nancy Okail, the Egyptian woman I mentioned at the beginning of the chapter who sat in my office relating the horrible events that had occurred over a span of just a few short months, bravely decided to return to her country to face trial.

When prosecutions begin in Egypt, the defendants appear in court in a cage. An actual cage. So much for a presumption of innocence. It was quite telling that in a press photo I came across of Nancy during that harrowing time, she was not shrinking. She was not visibly afraid. What was she doing instead? In the photo, she was reading George Orwell, perhaps trying to understand the authoritarian, thought-police drama she was ensconced in at that moment. (You can see the photo at http://www.vosizneias.com/news/photos/view/830245833.)

It brought a bittersweet smile to my face when I saw it. This persecuted woman, courageous yet afraid, aware of her role in this government drama, yet desperately trying to break free from this tyranny—for herself, her family, her country.

As of June 2012, Nancy decided to go back to stand trial in Egypt. As of this writing I do not know what will happen to her, but she is a hero and I hope her story will be told that way.

Another hero is Sherif Mansour.

Sherif was not in Egypt during the crackdown on his employer, Freedom House. He was in the United States. In fact, he was becoming a U.S. citizen—his lifelong dream.

But instead of simply continuing his work here and celebrating the freedoms he now enjoys as an American citizen, he returned to Egypt to stand beside Nancy and the other Egyptians as they undergo trial.

Sherif believes, and rightfully so, that most Americans have lost focus on this episode, since the American citizens were allowed to go free. He is hoping that his standing trial as an American citizen will help keep the public spotlight on the abuses of the Egyptian government.

I stand with him and with Nancy, and will continue to fight to demand reform in Egypt before we send them foreign aid.

In the past decade, much of our foreign policy has been America as the world's policeman, as a nation builder, or as a force to spread democracy and human rights.

America has always been a light and an example to the world. But there are practical limits to what we can expect to accomplish. I don't agree with a foreign policy that has led to us being cavalier in our use of force, that ignores the

Constitution and even basic common sense, around the world and in our name.

There is something to be said for America doing two important things—shining our beacon of freedom in places around the world in need of such illumination, but also not spending our time and treasure in countries that regularly thumb us in the eye.

We needn't bomb everyone who suppresses freedom. We can't afford it, and honestly, it wouldn't solve the problem. But we can use other tools at our disposal—foreign aid, or more accurately, withholding of foreign aid—to persuade other countries to follow the path toward more freedom. We can't afford to dole out any foreign aid at the moment, but as long as we are, why should we encourage countries that behave in a tyrannical manner by giving them American taxpayer dollars?

There are many reasons why I chose to write in this book about the Egyptian detainee situation. First, I wanted to note that bullying and abuse of power by a government is certainly not something unique to our government. Even with our problems, you certainly cannot really compare our government to that of a country like Egypt. Indeed, for most of our history and in countless ways, we have been one of the lesser offenders when it comes to government bullying and abuse.

All governments, at one time or another and to varying degrees, will assume too much power. They will cease following the rules written for them. They will attempt to trample on the rights of their citizens. From California to Cairo, this will inevitably happen. Such is the nature of government, and America always stands for liberty and against tyranny.

The other reason I wanted to write about this situation of Americans being detained is because at the time this was happening, Egypt was not the only place where the detention of

American citizens was being contemplated. In fact, while most of my colleagues were with me on this issue, and were not in favor of Egypt being allowed to detain Americans, they were also readily handing vast new powers of detention of American citizens to our federal government, and particularly the executive branch. This threat to our long-standing historic liberties came as part of something called the "National Defense Authorization Act."

Some of what this act contains will haunt every freedom-loving American. Some of it allows our government to take away some of the basic things that make us American.

The right to due process, habeas corpus, a fair trial—these are basic American rights enshrined in our Constitution that no branch of government has the right or power to take from us. The very concept of what we think of as "freedom" rests first on these basic legal precepts. Americans cannot stand idly by and watch their destruction. And we won't.

PART 4

★ ★ ★

Keeping Us Safe? FDA and USDA Bullies

"*Excessive bail shall not be required, nor excessive fines imposed, nor cruel and unusual punishments inflicted.*"

—United States Constitution, Amendment VIII

17

★ ★ ★

Paved with Good Intentions

"If people let the government decide what foods they eat and what medicines they take, their bodies will soon be in as sorry a state as the souls who live under tyranny."

—THOMAS JEFFERSON

* * *

Those who say that art and culture can't influence government don't know their history.

For America's first hundred years, we were mostly an agrarian nation. We only ate what we grew ourselves or what was grown nearby. Lacking the technology to preserve food, anything we grew or butchered for commercial purposes had to be sold quickly.

As technology advanced and America became more urban and industrialized, the demand for commercial food products grew—and so did the incidence of disease, deplorable industry conditions, unsafe production methods, and other problems for those who grew, processed, and shipped food.

Early-twentieth-century muckraking journalists regularly told horror stories in vivid detail about the emerging commercial food industry. Like most stories—in the long and "proud" history of sensationalist journalism—some of them were true and some were not. Some were half true.

Upton Sinclair's famous 1906 novel *The Jungle* was written to focus attention on the deplorable working conditions in Chicago's meatpacking district. Sinclair depicted immigrant workers' impoverishment and tragic existence. The author wanted to show the rest of America just how rough these new-comers to our country had it.

But the general public—and the federal government—took a different lesson from his book than perhaps Sinclair intended.

One of the stories in *The Jungle* depicts dangerous working conditions, and describes a scene where employees at a meat-packing plant fall into the "rendering pit" at their factory. The workers' bodies are mangled and ground up along with all of the other animal-parts. The final product is later put on the market as lard.

This story was never proved, and in fact was likely false. Though many of the horror stories depicted in the book were true—general poor health and safety conditions, abusive child labor—the story that was not provable created public demand for one of the largest expansions of government in history: the Food and Drug Administration and the national Department of Agriculture.

In 1906, President Theodore Roosevelt signed into law the Food and Drug Acts, creating what would later become the FDA (first known as the Bureau of Chemistry). These acts included nationwide food inspections, creating a new federal bureaucracy that cost $30 million in 1906.

As government inevitably does, these agencies and their missions expanded over the years. In 1938, President Franklin Roosevelt signed the Food, Drug, and Cosmetic Act, adding many provisions to the FDA's original mission, including regulation of mechanical devices and cosmetics. Basically, if you could ingest it or put it on your skin or hair, the FDA could now regulate it, and the agency could enforce these regulations by inspecting private businesses.

Prescription drug controls were tightened. The FDA demanded an approval process for all new drugs, testing for safety and efficacy. They set up new procedures for clinical trials and evaluations. Since 1938, the FDA has approved all drugs sold in the United States.

So far none of this should be cause for alarm. But as we all know, even government programs created with the best intentions can get out of control if they are allowed to grow unchecked. Government programs that begin in one era can take on new or different functions in a later era. Depending on the moment in history and on what the general public will tolerate at the time, these programs are more or less susceptible to being challenged or questioned. Today the FDA employs over eleven thousand people. It has requested a budget of $4.5 billion for fiscal year 2013—an increase of nearly 20 percent over FY 2012 allocations!

That massive amount funds just a part of the FDA's original mission. Today the FDA is part of the Department of Health and Human Services, and concentrates on regulating drugs and medical devices. The "food" part of the Food and Drug Administration—the entire reason for creating the FDA—for the most part doesn't exist anymore. That function is now mostly handled by the Department of Agriculture.

The USDA has existed in various forms since the early 1830s, but became officially the Department of Agriculture (a noncabinet agency at first) under President Lincoln. In 1889 the USDA finally became a full cabinet agency.

Like the FDA, the history of the USDA is again the inevitable tale of runaway government growth. As mentioned earlier, for the first hundred years of America's history, nearly our entire country and economy were based on agriculture.

Somehow we managed to get by without a federal department of agriculture. But with the passage of time, as our country became less based on agriculture, the government saw fit to intervene and "help" us.

The USDA in 2013 is expected to have a budget of over $150 billion. That's billion with a "b." That this agency is a monster is undeniable. That it has grown out of proportion to our actual need for it, not to mention its original purpose, is also undeniable.

The USDA employs over 100,000 workers throughout the United States and even in foreign countries. What do these workers do? Some "help" farmers. They don't actually pick crops, mind you. They administer price support and loan programs, which most farmers will tell you are out of date. They handle food safety. They staff the Forest Service.

I think we can all agree that there is a need and a role for an agency like the USDA, though with fewer employees and less taxpayer dollars—*a lot* fewer employees and less taxpayer dollars.

So what happens to an agency with a well-intended mission that bloats to 100,000 employees and a $150 billion budget? It starts to look for new missions. It starts to find new purposes. It starts to believe it can do basically whatever the heck it wants to do.

Again, one wouldn't think that such agencies would have a need for automatic weapons and SWAT teams, perfectly willing to terrorize farmers, organic food co-ops, and natural food stores across the country.

For centuries, Amish and Mennonite communities have farmed the hilly countryside of Pennsylvania. They've used the same methods and practices for just as long. These communities have often supplied the same families and stores.

Until about ten years ago, they did so largely without interference from the federal government. Not anymore. Now small farmers up and down the Mid-Atlantic region are raided at gunpoint by goons from the USDA and FDA. What product were they trafficking in that led to such harsh treatment from their government?

Milk.

That's right, mostly milk. We can add this to guitars and bunnies to create quite a bizarre list of contraband items seized by overzealous government agents.

Our government is trying to put the small organic dairy farmer out of business. They bully farmers with the full cooperation of state agriculture departments, which use the same tactics against farmers.

I'll tell you the story of a co-op in Kentucky that ran afoul of the state Agriculture Department. I'll tell you the story of a natural food store in California. I'll tell you the story of an Amish farmer in Pennsylvania.

These stories span the length of the country. They involve different methods of farming and delivery, and different types of businesses, but they all had one thing in common: The offenders dared to sell raw milk to willing, informed consumers.

In November 2011, my office was happy to participate with the Raw Milk Freedom Riders, who set out to acquire raw milk in protest of raids on small farmers like Dan Allgyer of Pennsylvania.

The Raw Milk Freedom Riders intentionally purchased

and transported raw milk across state lines in violation of federal law. They set up shop right outside the FDA headquarters in Silver Spring, Maryland. Then they drove to a farm in Pennsylvania, acquired the raw milk, and headed back across the state line to Maryland. Once everyone arrived, the "illegal" milk was distributed to waiting protesters, who sat and listened to various speakers while eating homemade cookies (probably some other sort of FDA or USDA regulation was broken there as well).

The speakers came from across the country, and each had had all sorts of different horrible experiences with the FDA and USDA.

Organizer Liz Reitzig, president of the Maryland Independent Consumers and Farmers Association and cofounder of the Farm Food Freedom Coalition, made the point that the FDA ban on raw milk undermines our own liberty, parental authority, and consumer choice, all for no good reason.

Kristin Canty and Sally Fallon Morrell, a nutrition expert, spoke about the health benefits of raw milk. Ms. Canty believes that raw milk cured her son of severe allergies, and he is now a healthy teenager, allergy- and medication-free. Canty produced a documentary called *Farmaggedon*, which highlighted the government raids, abuse, and overzealous regulation of family farms. Anyone who sees it would be scared out of their wits, knowing what government is empowered to do to farmers on your behalf.

A leader of the farm freedom movement, Joel Salatin, also spoke at the rally. Joel is a farmer and author from Virginia, who noted that the government allows kids to ingest Mountain Dew, Twinkies, and Cocoa Puffs but finds raw milk to be a health threat to worry about. Joel makes an excellent point.

Mark McAfee, owner of Organic Pastures Dairy Company in California, spoke at the rally. Although raw milk is technically legal in California, he was investigated (undercover) in 2004 and 2007.

Pete Kennedy of the Farm-to-Consumer Legal Defense Fund outlined a lawsuit his organization was filing, challenging the interstate ban in a federal district court.

The speaker who came from the farthest away to participate was Michael Schmidt, a dairy farmer from Ontario, Canada. For the past twenty years, Mr. Schmidt has been selling raw milk through a cow share program. But in 2006, armed agents raided his farm, arrested him, and put him in jail. He was prosecuted for fifteen counts of distributing unpasteurized milk.

Mr. Schmidt, despite his prosecution, is still an advocate for food freedom. In fact, at the day of the rally he was on the thirty-fourth day of a hunger strike, in an attempt to get Canada's premier to meet with him to discuss the sale of safe raw milk.

Civil disobedience. Hunger strikes. Persecuted activists. The food freedom movement has all the hallmarks of the great struggles of the past, and that's because it shares a common enemy with those movements—aggressive and arrogant government.

More Americans than ever are standing up to fight and take action.

Carolyn Moffa from my Senate staff proudly participated and drank some of the "illegal" milk. So far she hasn't been arrested. But isn't it insane to think that in America someone could be arrested for the "crime" of drinking milk directly from the cow?

Interestingly, among the participants in the rally was

someone from my own state of Kentucky—a constituent from Louisville who has been investigated and attacked by our state agriculture authorities. I wouldn't have even known about that if not for the rally. I'll tell you a bit more about him too.

These people share one thing in common—they want to be left alone. They aren't just conservatives or liberals, or Democrats or Republicans. They come from different backgrounds, live in different states, and have divergent political beliefs on other issues.

But they all want freedom. They know it is being taken away. And they are fighting to take their government back. When I ran for office, I said I would stand with folks just like them. And I do.

18

★ ★ ★

Public Enemy No. 1: Amish Raw Milk

"I'm for regulation, but why is the FDA doing this? Here's the FDA in hazmat suits taking on the little farmer with twenty cows. This is an Amish guy trying to make a living."

—MARION NESTLE, NUTRITIONIST

Imagine that it is 5 a.m. on a hazy morning in April. The sun has not yet risen and you are still in bed, resting and thinking about the laborious day ahead working on your farm. But instead of being wakened by your alarm clock, you are yanked out of bed by a government agent. Imagine your day beginning with an unannounced government raid—two U.S. marshals and a state trooper, storming your farm with a warrant and loaded weapons in hand.

You would no doubt be wondering what you had done wrong, how this abrupt intrusion had come about and why. Yet you would soon learn that you had been the target of a yearlong sting operation conducted by the federal government.

This might sound like the trailer for some upcoming action movie. It is not. It is precisely what happened to Amish farmer Daniel Allgyer.

Daniel Allgyer, his wife, Rachel, and their eight children live in a town called Kinzers in Lancaster County, Pennsylvania. Like most Amish families, they live simple lives while operating their dairy farm, Rainbow Acres Farm. They run a small agricultural business from their farm, where they sell fresh cheese, butter, milk, and produce. You might be wondering what made the seemingly innocent Amish dairy farmer

Allgyer a target worthy of federal search and seizure. Was Mr. Allgyer committing violent crimes? Was he selling drugs from his home? Was he housing criminals?

No, Daniel Allgyer was selling fresh raw milk to hundreds of buyers throughout the Northeast. Amish dairy farms operate under the guidelines of *Ordnung*, a set of rules long accepted and obeyed by the Amish community. The guidelines include certain limitations on everyday living and prohibit or limit the use of power-line electricity, telephones, automobiles, and modern dress. The Amish live their daily lives without many of the modern technological conveniences most Americans have come to rely on. Due to these simple standards of living, it should be no surprise that the dairy products produced by Rainbow Acres Farm were not pasteurized or treated with modern production methods. Their milk was raw.

The raw milk market is a significant one—there are over ten million raw milk consumers in our country. Mr. Allgyer was a very well-known and well-respected dairy farmer throughout the Northeast. Countless people depended on his farm for their dairy. Liz Reitzig began buying raw milk from Allgyer when her daughter was having a hard time digesting pasteurized milk. She became a regular customer of Rainbow Acres Farm, saying, "We like the way they farm, we love their product. It is super-high-quality and they are wonderful. It is just a wonderful arrangement."

But the Food and Drug Administration disagrees—the agency does not think the sale of raw milk is wonderful. In fact, this federal agency has gone to extreme measures to make acquiring this product incredibly difficult.

In 1987, the FDA banned the interstate sale of raw milk.

Since then, the agency has vowed to do everything it can to regulate this business. If it was within the FDA's jurisdiction, the agency would ban the sale of raw milk altogether. "It is the FDA's position that raw milk should never be consumed," said Tamara N. Ward, spokeswoman for the FDA.

There are potential problems if a corporation wanted to distribute raw milk nationally, but these problems don't necessarily apply to family businesses, farms, and co-ops that distribute and share at local, state, and regional levels. No one is saying we should mass-produce raw milk commercially. The FDA fails to recognize this important distinction.

The agency insists on taking a strong stance opposing the sale of raw milk. A stance so strong that the FDA saw fit to spend taxpayer dollars to fund a yearlong sting operation to prosecute an Amish dairy farmer. The food freedom blog hartkeisonline.com described Allgyer's operation:

> Federal regulators often cite food safety concerns to justify their actions that shut down private enterprises. Let's look at Dan Allgyer's track record. At the time of his farm's closure, he was farming around 100 acres. He provided an impressive range of nutrient dense foods to his club members: raw milk, grass-fed meats, soy-free chickens/eggs to nearly 500 families. *Never, in 6 years, did a club member report a food borne illness from trading directly with Dan* [emphasis added].

According to the ten-page complaint that was filed against Allgyer, the FDA began to investigate Rainbow Acres Farm in late 2009. An investigator located in Baltimore used aliases to sign up for a Yahoo! user group for Rainbow Acres' customers. The investigator began placing orders for raw milk and would have these orders delivered to a private residence in Maryland.

Because the orders were being sent from the Pennsylvania farm to a residence in Maryland, it became a federal violation and thus—you guessed it—under the jurisdiction of the FDA. This was the plan from the beginning of this sting operation— that by crossing state lines, the distribution of the milk would come under the interstate commerce clause, thus making Daniel Allgyer a lawbreaker. After months of surveillance, investigators visited Rainbow Acres Farm. Allgyer turned them away, telling them they did not have the proper documentation to search his property. This angered the FDA, so they returned two months later, at the crack of dawn, with a warrant and weapons in tow to startle and arrest Mr. Allgyer. Pete Kennedy, president of the Farm-to-Consumer Legal Defense, tells us that "[undercover sting operations] happen quite a bit. It is almost like they treat raw milk as crack. It has happened in a number of states and at the federal level."

During the raid of Rainbow Acres Farm, investigators found coolers labeled "to be delivered" to various towns in Maryland. This raid led to a cease-and-desist order from the FDA. The agency demanded that Allgyer stop selling his dairy products across state lines. But instead of ceasing all business, Allgyer formed a club of sorts. He made customers sign an agreement stating that they supported and understood the operations of his farm and were not trying to entrap the owners, and he qualified all members to become shareholders in the farm's produce, paying only for the farmer's labor. Raw milk advocates hoped this agreement would allow Rainbow Acres to evade the FDA's definition of "commerce," thus tak-

ing the matter out of the federal government's purview altogether. You cannot have commerce with yourself. If you are a
part owner in the cow in question, then the commerce clause
doesn't apply—you are simply receiving what is already yours.

Not surprisingly, this tactic didn't save Allgyer from the
FDA's wrath. The agency filed suit against Rainbow Acres
Farm. Judge Lawrence F. Stengel ruled that Allgyer could no
longer ship raw milk to other states. Most of Allgyer's customers reside outside Pennsylvania, so due to this court ruling he
was required to shut down his farm. Putting Rainbow Acres
Farm out of business was the FDA's ultimate goal throughout
this entire saga.

This case goes far beyond the debate about the health factors that come with consuming raw milk. This prosecution by
the FDA and ruling by Judge Lawrence completely disregards
individual liberties. This scenario acts as proof that the FDA
now has jurisdiction over private property use. A Rainbow
Acres Farm customer describes this outrageous situation, stating his disbelief: "I cannot believe in 2012 our federal government is raiding Amish farmers at gunpoint all over a basic
human right to eat natural food. In Maryland they force taxpayers to fund abortions, but God forbid we want to drink the
same raw milk that our grandparents and great-grandparents
drank."

19

★ ★ ★

State and Local Bullies

"The only power any government has is the power to crack down on criminals. Well, when there aren't enough criminals, one makes them. One declares so many things to be a crime that it becomes impossible for men to live without breaking laws."

—AYN RAND

Last fall, a constituent of mine from Louisville traveled all the way to Maryland to have his voice heard. John Moody was going to be part of a raw milk rally that was being held in Silver Spring outside the Food and Drug Administration's headquarters.

We've spent a lot of time in this book talking about the federal government. As the stories attest, these criticisms are just and necessary. It should be obvious by now that an overwhelming amount of the trouble caused by government is caused by the federal agencies—unelected and uncontrollable bureaucrats who've bestowed upon themselves the power to dictate the most intimate details of our daily lives.

But state and local governments are certainly not blameless. They are not immune to the government trend of stated agency missions suddenly changing, with power always growing, and the arrogance of that power taking them further down the path toward authoritarianism and unaccountability.

My constituent, John Moody, came to D.C. to fight for others. Luckily, he was not under any federal investigation or prosecution. But he did have a story to tell about Kentucky.

In 2004, with several other families, John founded Louisville Whole Life, a buying club, in which the participants worked together with small local farms to distribute raw milk, fresh eggs, and other natural products to their members.

Harmless enough, right? Not according to the FDA.

The FDA first started going after raw milk producers by stopping them from selling directly to consumers across state lines. The agency was able to successfully stretch its logic to claim jurisdiction in regulating such commerce.

But farm freedom advocates figured out a way around this. Absolutely nothing in federal law can or would stop a person from receiving milk from a cow he or she owns, or eggs from a chicken that belongs to them. So these enterprising folks set up partial ownership of the animal itself. The farmer sold a "share" in the cow. Each person owned part of it, and was therefore entitled to a certain amount of milk from that cow. The milk was technically not being sold at all. For members who wanted raw milk, it was "their" cow. The practice is popular not only back home in Kentucky, but in and around Washington, D.C., and many other places across the country.

Louisville Whole Life grew, creating twenty good-paying jobs and reaching about a thousand people each week with fresh farm-to-home products. Members of the buying club sign private contracts. They pay an annual fee that gives them a share in the livestock and access to other products from the farms. They are then able to take delivery of these products legally, which is their own property under the law.

Mr. Moody was very clear in his discussion of his business in Kentucky, telling everyone at the rally that he faced a "hostile regulatory environment" for farmers and consumers. The outright sale of raw milk is illegal, except for goat's milk for some reason. However, specific language in the Kentucky constitution dealing with property rights and private contracts appears to apply to cow and herd shares.

It should surprise no one that federal laws that are vague and nonsensical are mirrored at the state level.

On May 27, 2011, without any prior contact or warning, Louisville Whole Life was slapped with a cease-and-desist order from the Louisville Metro Department of Public Health and Wellness and, at the same time, a separate quarantine order from the Kentucky Cabinet for Health and Family Services. Note that it took two separate government agencies working in conjunction with one another—and no doubt with months of bureaucratic coordination—to stop *just one* small raw milk dealer. Fifty gallons of raw milk were promptly seized and labeled as "quarantined."

Mr. Moody spoke with the members and administrators of the club and drafted a response citing Articles 1, 2, 4, 10, 19, and 26 of the Kentucky constitution as the legal defense for their club.

When members came to pick up their milk—which they did in violation of the government orders—they signed the document, declaring the milk to be their property, as part of the agreement. By the end of this process, more than a hundred Kentucky citizens had signed the document, stood up to their government, and left proudly, liberty intact, with their "quarantined" milk.

There was a good deal of local media attention following the incident, and the government took notice. State and local governments received a barrage of calls from Kentuckians in support of these farm freedom advocates.

In this case, public pressure worked. Both the local and

state offices withdrew their complaints, removed their quarantines, and disposed of their cease-and-desist orders.

Mr. Moody was kind enough to cite my election as a galvanizing event for foes of obtrusive government. He noted the activism that began in the Tea Party, continued in my 2010 antiestablishment campaign, and marched forward through those who took up just causes in their fight against regulatory absurdity. In Kentucky, food freedom was unquestionably one of those causes.

So popular was this cause with Kentuckians that Moody was contacted by both 2011 Republican candidates for governor, who after reading his story wanted to offer their help. One of those candidates, David Williams, is now Kentucky's state senate president and has plans to push a raw milk freedom bill through my state's legislature.

But such victories are rare concerning food freedom across the nation, and they are virtually unheard of concerning our out-of-control FDA.

In fact, Mr. Moody told me he had no idea that the publicity he helped generate might have an unintended consequence, as he wondered aloud to me whether he would find himself under federal investigation as Dan Allgyer had been.

Who knows? Our government operates without rhyme or reason at multiple levels.

John Moody still wonders today, not without reason, if perhaps his battle is not yet over.

20

★ ★ ★

Cute and Fuzzy Bunnies

"We're going to make an example of you."
—USDA SPOKESMAN

* * *

What do government programs and rabbits have in common? If you leave them alone, they breed. Quickly.

In one of the sadder cases I've seen in recent years, rabbits and bureaucratic bullies became part of the same government mix—to the grave detriment of taxpayers, the rabbits of concern, and a young family in Missouri.

I wanted to tell this story for an important reason. Sometimes when people hear that someone has run afoul of the EPA or some other government organization, they have one of two immediate reactions:

- Those who believe that government is too large and intrusive automatically assume that the agency is out of control and out to hurt the business; or
- Those with a more liberal perspective toward government size and power might think, "Well, the person under investigation owns a coal mine, or a shopping center, or a big patch of land they want to develop." They envision the caricature of a robber baron, assuming that whatever the property owner is accused of, they're likely guilty and the government is justified in trying to keep big business under control.

But what about when the government interferes with small family businesses and ordinary citizens? That interference becomes bullying in the worst sense: when farms are raided, lemonade stands are shut down—and teenagers selling bunnies are fined $3.9 million.

That's right, $3.9 million for selling bunnies.

At our "Property Wrongs" Senate hearing in 2011, I met the Dollarhite family, who testified before our committee. They struck me as a close, happy family, probably similar to most of the readers of this book. They never intended to roil or oppose their government. In fact, it isn't clear they set out with much of a plan at all, certainly no mischievous one.

The Dollarhites live in Nixa, Missouri, on three agriculturally zoned acres. Husband and wife John and Judy have a background in agriculture and wanted to give their teenage son a real life lesson in the family business. In 2006, the couple rescued two rabbits. Soon, as rabbits inevitably and rapidly do, their new rabbits began reproducing. The Dollarhites decided handling these rabbits would be a good first business project for their son. He would raise and care for the rabbits and then sell the meat by the pound, or perhaps sell the rabbits as pets to their neighbors and friends. This was supposed to be the rabbit version of a lemonade stand, something to teach their son the value of hard work, responsibility, and the trials and tribulations of the agriculture business.

Being from an agricultural background, the Dollarhites also knew that there must be some regulatory process monitored by the U.S. Department of Agriculture. John Dollarhite went to the USDA office and was told by agency representatives that they only dealt with water and soil issues. After being directed and shuffled around to dozens of various government officials, they were advised to call the USDA regional office in Colorado Springs. The regional office told the Dollarhites that they did not need a USDA license because the government classified rabbits as poultry and thus did not regulate them. They were surprised by this information and wanted to be extra sure they were following the proper rules and procedures, so they continued to seek answers. They attended church with a USDA meat inspector, who confirmed that the USDA did not regulate poultry.

So, finally, the Dollarhites began their business of selling rabbits.

The Dollarhites' rabbits became quickly widely known and sold by the dozen. They were praised by experts for their superior quality and condition. The Dollarhites launched a business website and put a sign in their yard advertising rabbits for sale. Still, the overwhelming majority of their customers came due to word of mouth. "We started becoming the go-to people for rabbits in the Springfield area," said John Dollarhite. If locals or people from across the state wanted a rabbit, they would go to the "Dollarvalue Rabbitry," he explained.

The rabbitry became so renowned that in 2009 two very large buyers approached the family. Local theme park Silver Dollar City wished to purchase rabbits to sell in their petting zoo. National pet store chain Petland wished to sell the family's rabbits as well, and also asked the Dollarhites to raise and sell guinea pigs to the pet chain, because they were having difficulty acquiring both animals from their other suppliers.

By the end of 2009, the Dollarhites had sold approximately 440 rabbits and grossed $4,600, with a profit of approximately $200. John said that that profit was enough to provide the family with pocket money, which enabled them to eat out at a restaurant on a couple of occasions. It never entered their minds that they were doing anything wrong, especially since they reported their income and took only their allowed deductions on their tax returns.

In the fall of 2009, the Dollarhites decided to downsize their rabbitry operations. Their son had lost interest and Judy Dollarhite's father needed to be placed in a nursing home and she would become his guardian. Shortly after the downsizing began, the Dollarhites received a visit from the USDA. An inspector showed up at the family's home, unannounced, without a warrant, without citation, and without any identification. The official claimed that she was there to conduct a "spot inspection" of the rabbitry. After scouring the premises, she declared that everything seemed to be in order and that their rabbits were some of the healthiest she had inspected. The inspector did say that there were a few minor and insignificant aspects of the facility that were in violation of USDA standards, but the Dollarhites were not certified by the USDA, nor were they required to be. The USDA official asked if the Dollarhites were interested in becoming USDA-certified and they informed the agent that they would look into it. That was the end of the government inspection.

Or so they thought.

The Dollarhites carried on with their daily business until January 2010, when the USDA returned. The family received a phone call from a Kansas City–based USDA inspector who requested to have a meeting with the family regarding their rabbitry. The official informed them that refusing to meet with him would be a huge mistake and advised them to have an attorney present. During the meeting they were advised to cease their rabbit business, and if they did so, they would only face up to $1,000 in fines. The USDA agent explained that they should expect a four- to six-week time frame for the report to be filed, and then they could expect to hear the USDA's decision.

The Dollarhites followed the advice of the agent and immediately closed their business. They traded all of their stock, cages, and equipment for other agricultural items and they made changes to their website, explaining that they were no longer in the rabbit business. But after eight weeks had passed, they had still not received any sort of notification from the USDA.

So John Dollarhite became proactive, calling the agency in order to find out its verdict. USDA enforcement specialist Roxanne Folk received John's call. Dollarhite said she was very short with him. Folk told Mr. Dollarhite that their file was sitting on her desk and she had not finished reviewing it. She added harshly that they should expect to be prosecuted to the full extent of the law and that the USDA was going to make "an example" out of them. When John asked what she meant by that, Folk stated that they would simply have to wait for notification from her, then she promptly hung up the phone.

The Dollarhites did not hear from the USDA for an entire year.

Then in April 2011 the Dollarhites received a certified letter in the mail claiming that they had violated the Animal Welfare Act. Their fine? *$3.9 million!* But the USDA, in its benevolent mercy, informed the family that the agency was willing to settle for a payment of $90,643 if paid by May 23, 2011—a mere month later.

So what exactly could the Dollarhites have possibly done to deserve such a draconian fine?

They had violated some mystery law that prohibits the

selling of more than $500 worth of rabbits within a one-year period. Even though the Dollarhites were in full accordance with Missouri state law and did not sell their rabbits to other states—the business was carefully conducted on their private and spacious residence and the rabbits were kept in large, clean, and well-maintained cages—their business was still subjected to the grasp of bureaucracy run amok.

At the advice of their attorney, the Dollarhites have told their story of injustice to anyone who will listen, from the media to members of Congress. After several Senate and congressional offices, along with countless citizens, exerted pressure, the Dollarhites received a further reply from the USDA. The agency informed them that if they agreed to an inspection of their property to verify that they no longer had rabbits, the USDA would drop the fine without penalty. The Dollarhites immediately agreed and two USDA officials promptly arrived for the inspection. The inspection lasted no longer than seven minutes and the inspectors said they were satisfied with what they saw.

Just when the Dollarhites thought this tragedy was over, the government struck again. On June 22, 2011, the Dollarhites received a letter from the USDA stating that the family must agree to never again own any breeding animals of any kind, thus disqualifying them from ever obtaining a USDA license. This was not part of the inspection agreement as had been discussed previously. So in July the Dollarhites responded by saying that they had cleared the inspection and agreed not to raise rabbits for resale. But they stood up for their constitutional rights and refused to be treated differently than any other American citizen.

This was government bullying defined: Bureaucrats shouldn't

be able to dictate what type of livestock or pets the Dollarhites could or could not own.

Upon receiving the Dollarhites' letter, Bernadette Juarez, deputy director of the USDA, called and demanded that they sign the previous agreement. This agreement included a clause that banned them from owning pets for the next five years. In response to this imperious phone call, the Dollarhites' attorney requested that Juarez submit the agency's requirements and requests in writing. Juarez agreed to do so by the close of business that day. To this day and as of this writing—well over a year later—the Dollarhites have yet to receive any written statement from the USDA.

The Dollarhites currently live in a perpetual state of bureaucrat-enforced limbo. This entire scenario proves once again that these arrogant bureaucratic agencies are a constant and wildly unpredictable threat to our personal liberties and constitutional rights.

After getting to know the Dollarhites and their story, I've worked feverishly with other Capitol Hill leaders to make sure no American ever has to go through what they did. I've introduced legislation such as the REINS Act to help return the oversight of these regulatory agencies to Congress, which is our constitutional duty to begin with. We introduced legislation to prevent USDA agents from carrying weapons. The last thing we need is an armed bunny Gestapo harassing family farmers across the country.

The USDA's lust for power and control over our personal and private lives is unjust and un-American. We Americans won't stand for it.

21

★ ★ ★

How Can We Solve
the Problem?

"Politics is the art of looking for trouble, finding it everywhere, diagnosing it incorrectly, and applying the wrong remedies."

—GROUCHO MARX

* * *

I believe that the fight for food and health freedom is one of the most important battles our country and the liberty movement will face over the next decade.

It used to be simple. Food was grown locally. Methods were similar to those of modern organic farms. "Fresh" was easy to find, chemicals were rare, and processing was minimal.

For many reasons, this is the ideal method of food delivery and ingestion for human beings. This is the way we are supposed to produce and consume food. Still, the old-fashioned concept of family farms and local agriculture isn't necessarily practical for a nation of 300 million people spread across three thousand miles of land.

People want solutions. Those who enjoy and have come to depend on raw milk want it to be legal for consenting consumers to purchase. I share their concern, but we must also be realistic in our goals. We cannot nor should we expect every Safeway or Kroger in America to stock raw milk. In fact, mass-produced raw milk probably would not be safe.

But the milk you buy from the Amish farmer in the next county? Or the milk from the Maryland farm that offers next-day delivery to Washington, D.C.? Big difference.

My father-in-law Hilton Ashby grew up on a little farm in

Lewisburg, Kentucky, drinking raw milk straight from the cow (you can ask him about how the milk tasted when the cow ate too many onions). Today, at eighty-one, Hilton has survived pretty well drinking raw milk.

And this has been the way most Americans have consumed milk for as long as there has been an America. It has always been our choice. We should still have that choice.

These days our huge government isn't too big on choice. As of this writing, a major American city is contemplating banning sugary drinks over sixteen ounces. Why sixteen ounces? Who knows. The point is, the government inherently thinks it knows whether you should be allowed to purchase sixteen ounces, eighteen ounces, two liters—you get the picture. Our government believes it must police every vitamin and supplement Americans take. It really shouldn't surprise anyone that the government thinks it should be the sole determiner of whether or not Americans can drink raw milk.

There are two major problems with the FDA and USDA today. The first is their inflated and arrogant sense of jurisdiction— what they think they should be able to control. Secondly, these agencies have SWAT teams and undercover agents capable of conducting nighttime raids on private property owners, often to flex their bureaucratic muscle and exercise their control.

Both problems are unacceptable. I've introduced several bills to rein in the government's war on natural foods, supplements, raw milk, and those who grow, sell, or consume these products.

I have introduced a bill to make the sale of raw milk legal throughout the United States. I must admit, I don't drink raw milk. My staff often laughs at my negative reaction to it, and in explaining that reaction, I've told stories of my grandparents' dairy in Pennsylvania. The milk my grandparents sold was local, fresh, and pasteurized. For them, it was simply the most foolproof way to deliver milk to a large population.

So that's what I grew up drinking. But many Americans have been raised drinking raw milk, including many of my constituents in Kentucky. I choose not to drink raw milk, and that's my choice. But those who want to should have that choice too. That's the entire point. You don't have to be an advocate for raw milk, or agree that it is inherently superior, to be an advocate for consumer choice, business choice, and farmer choice.

Another bill I've introduced is called the Health Freedom Act, which would protect vitamin and supplement manufacturers from some of the current unreasonable government regulations. The burden of proof of wrongdoing should lie not with private business but with the government. As the Constitution demands, if the government wants to raid your office, shut down your business, and harass you and your customers, it should have to prove its case to a judge first.

An interesting aspect of working in the Senate is a senator's unique ability to affect day-to-day debate, even as a freshman member like myself who is known for often holding minority views.

None of the bills I have mentioned in this chapter could pass through the current Congress. We are well short of the necessary defenders of liberty in the Senate to pass such legislation. In the House, this means that my bills and issues would not see the light of day. They would never be debated. No floor action would be taken, no votes held, no advancement of the issues we care about.

But in the U.S. Senate, one senator can stand up and say, "Stop." I can offer amendments and insist on their consideration. Now, this power is not absolute, nor should it be—my colleagues can essentially run over me if they are willing to invest the necessary time to do so. But such blocking by other senators would often take the better part of a week or more, because of complicated Senate rules—rules that I learned, and insisted my staff learn, from the moment I arrived in Washington.

This is exactly how I fired the first legislative shot across the bow of the FDA and their deplorable police-state tactics.

In the summer of 2012, I blocked an FDA-related bill in order to force a discussion and a vote on an amendment to rein in the agency. My amendment was designed to address the rogue nature and tyrannical tactics of agencies like the FDA, as demonstrated by the stories I'm sharing with you in this book.

I think most Americans are troubled by the notion of armed FDA agents raiding peaceful Amish farmers for the "crime" of selling milk directly from the cow. Unfortunately, this is not the only assault on freedom we've seen coming from the Food and Drug Administration.

My amendment had three parts.

First, it attempted to stop the FDA's overzealous regulation of vitamins, food, and supplements. It also addressed the fact that the FDA has been in the censorship business for years. The First Amendment guarantees our right to free speech, and this should include vitamin and supplement manufacturers, who have every right to advertise beneficial health information, whether the FDA approves of it or not.

Major corporations who manufacture vitamins and supplements are often able to advertise certain health benefits. Walk into any health food or vitamin store and you can find shelves full of products promising all sorts of things beneficial to our physical well-being.

But what about the small businesses? What about those who sell and promote natural foods and supplements, products that are widely known to have certain health benefits, but the FDA doesn't think these businesses should be allowed to advertise these benefits?

For millions of Americans suffering from a wide range of diseases or other health care problems, the FDA has regularly denied information regarding the therapeutic benefits of using dietary supplements. This is information Americans are entitled to know.

In their infinite wisdom, the FDA has even tried to protect Americans from Cheerios. Yes, that's right—in 2009, the FDA told the Cheerios manufacturer General Mills to cease and desist publicizing studies that showed eating the cereal may help lower cholesterol. Lawyer Mark Senak, who works regularly with pharmaceutical companies that are trying to bring new drugs to market, discussed this incident on his Eye on FDA blog (eyeonfda.com): "The FDA issued a Warning Letter to General Mills because of the promotional claims on a box of Cheerios. Here is what the FDA said—'Based on claims made on your product's label [the box], we have determined that your Cheerios Toasted Whole Wheat Grain Cereal is promoted for conditions that *cause it to be a drug* because the product is intended for use in the prevention, mitigation and treatment of disease' [emphasis my own]. I bet you didn't know that if you ate Cheerios."

The FDA's dictum against Cheerios did not stick, but the

absurdity of the agency, in the minds of many, certainly did. As Senak put it: "Speaking for myself, I don't think this type of action helps re-establish the FDA's credibility."

Currently, the FDA also makes it illegal for sellers of prune juice and similar juices to advertise that their product helps relieve constipation. *Natural News* is a good source for keeping track of the FDA's outrageous behavior. Reported *Natural News* in 2011: Wyldewood Cellars, a Kansas-based producer and distributor of elderberry juice, is the latest target of the agency, which recently sent U.S. marshals to the company's winery in Mulvane to confiscate the "unapproved drug...John Brewer, co-founder of Wyldewood, says that after receiving the initial FDA warning letter, his company hired a consultant familiar with FDA regulations to help his company reword their product descriptions. After making the appropriate changes, and clarifying that the elderberry products in question were supplements, Brewer says his company had done what it needed to in order to be in compliance. 'We haven't heard anything from [the FDA] since,' he told reporters."

Natural News describes how what happened to Wyldewood Cellars is a recurring theme: "This tactic, of course, has become all too common in recent years. A company receives a warning letter from the FDA, makes the appropriate changes, never hears anything further from the FDA, and out of nowhere gets raided... 'You think you are doing things correctly, and there hasn't been any word, and all of a sudden you get this,' said Brewer."

Maybe a little prune juice surreptitiously added to FDA employee coffee mugs would loosen up their regulations?

My amendment would have stopped the FDA from censoring claims about the curative, mitigative, or preventative effects of dietary supplements. It also would have stopped the FDA from prohibiting the distribution of scientific articles and publications regarding the role of nutrients in protecting against disease. Despite four court orders condemning the practice as a violation of the First Amendment, the FDA continues to deny certain health information, thus suppressing consumers' rights to make informed choices. It is time for Congress to put an end to such unnecessary and insane censorship by the FDA.

Second, my amendment would have disarmed the FDA by preventing agents from carrying firearms when executing warrants, arrests, or seizures of harmful products. Frankly, I don't want to see any more Amish farms raided with guns for the "crime" of selling raw milk from a cow. I think that's ludicrous, and I think most Americans agree. And quite frankly, it gives me the creeps to see armed federal agents invade someone's private property in such a jackbooted manner. Such things simply aren't supposed to happen in America.

Unfortunately, these are not isolated incidents. In 2011, *Natural News* complied a timeline of FDA raids on raw milk farmers, dietary supplement makers and natural medicine practitioners over the last quarter century. Starting in 1985, they cited 56 separate incidents, the premises of which would outrage most Americans—with the FDA barging into private businesses and seizing everything from materials and computer files to checkbooks and cash. This is insane.

I think we have too many armed federal agencies. Nearly forty different federal agencies can carry guns. We have too many agencies featuring armed agents because we have too many federal criminal laws. Criminal law is increasingly used as a tool by government to punish and control honest businessmen attempting to make a living. Historically, criminal law was intended to punish only the most horrible offenses, legitimate crimes that virtually everyone would agree were inherently evil or wrongful—murder, rape, theft, arson, and the like.

But today the criminal law is used to punish behavior such as fishing without a permit, packaging a product incorrectly, or shipping something with an "improper" label. This is absurd. The plain language of our Constitution specifies a very limited number of federal crimes. Originally, there were only four— treason, counterfeiting, piracy or felonies on the high seas, and offenses against the laws of nations.

But we have now moved so far away from the original intent of our Constitution that we don't even know or have a complete list of all the federal criminal laws on the books. There are over 4,450 federal statutory crimes scattered throughout the U.S. Code. It is estimated that there are tens of thousands more crimes that exist among all our federal regulations. But no one—not even criminal law professors or criminal lawyers—actually knows the exact number with certainty.

In addition to the unknown number of federal crimes, the vast majority of criminal statutes that have been passed by Congress in recent years lack adequate mens rea requirements—our traditional and basic legal notion of criminal intent. In other words, Congress passes laws that either completely lack or have an extremely weak "guilty mind" requirement, meaning that someone charged under the statute could be convicted of a federal offense when he or she just made an honest mistake, or perhaps did not possess the criminal intent traditionally necessary for a criminal conviction.

To address this, the third section of my amendment attempted to fix a small part of this enormous problem: It would have strengthened the mens rea component of each of the prohibited acts in the federal Food, Drug, and Cosmetic Act by including the words "knowing and willful" before each of the prohibitions. This is vitally important. If Congress is going to criminalize conduct at the federal level as it does in the Food, Drug, and Cosmetic Act, then the least it can do is include an adequate mens rea component. My amendment attempted to do just that.

My idea is to combine into one argument our fight for food freedom, health freedom, and freedom from the tyranny of overzealous federal agencies with SWAT teams. It will not surprise readers that this amendment failed. But we will never succeed if we don't begin fighting these battles. We cannot shrink or be timid in the face of creeping federal intrusion into our lives. Our federal government certainly isn't shy or timid.

There are folks all over America, from natural food suppliers in California to Amish farmers in Pennsylvania, who are heroes. They stand up against power much greater than their own. They fight for what they believe in against unbelievable odds and at considerable personal risk.

To the extent that I am able in my capacity as a U.S. senator, I will always have their back.

I hope you will too.

Conclusion

A friend of mine who helped edit this book commented that throughout the editing process these stories made him extremely mad. As a seasoned political operative and writer, he didn't think he was capable of that kind of outrage anymore, at least not from mere words on a page. He thought he had seen and heard it all. Honestly, so had I.

Another friend noted that every time she read a chapter she thought to herself, "This is the worst story of them all!" Then she would read the next story and think, "This is even worse than the last story!" The stories in this book weren't specifically ordered from bad to worse, so I don't even know if this perception is true. But I do suspect the outrage from reading these stories does have a cumulative effect. It makes sense that anger would build reading these horror stories, one after the other.

I hope you also are mad and disappointed by these tragic stories. Not that I want you to annoy your family and neighbors with long diatribes about the government. That is not my purpose. But I think we all need to be more aware of what our government is doing. And with that awareness, I think we all need to be a little angrier with our government.

It is important what we do when we get mad. Some people just get louder. Some people yell through bullhorns and kick the television set. Some of this stuff makes people feel better about themselves, and that's fine. But it won't change a thing in this world.

What really matters is addressing the injustices committed by our government before our very eyes every day, many of which are outlined in this book. I have some specific ideas on how you can get involved. But what really matters is that you get involved—and that you do what works best for you.

Getting involved can be as simple as helping the people who've helped some of the victims in this book. There are groups that fight every day for justice, to win back our rights and to change the laws that allow government to abuse and harass citizens. At the end of the book, I've provided a partial list. The list also appears on www.governmentbullies.com, with links to these groups.

Join these groups. Contribute to them. Write about them. Publicize them.

You can also get involved in electoral politics. You can decide who will be your next mayor or city councilman. You can decide who will be your next congressman, senator, or president. You can choose the people who get to write the laws and enforce them. You can choose the leaders who get to appoint the people who write the regulations—who say whether or not your backyard is a wetland, or whether your milk can come from a particular cow or farm.

If you don't like the people who are making the laws right now, you have some choices.

First, you can become one of them. Run for local office. Run for Congress or Senate. Actually, I don't really recommend running for Senate—I have to tell you, some of these people up here on Capitol Hill are a little hard to take. Last week we spent four days arguing over whether or not we should vote, then we left without voting. After we left, the guy in charge of setting votes yelled about how we didn't vote. I'm not kidding. Being a U.S. senator is often confusing and maddening.

You can become involved in the local party or movement of your choice. Attend a rally to End the Fed or a Tea Party event. Property rights meetings. Food freedom rallies. There are many organizations dedicated to whatever cause you believe needs the most focus. Get informed, volunteer to knock on doors and make calls for the person or organization that best represents your views.

I came to Washington eighteen months ago knowing I could not change the world immediately. But I thought I could make at least some headway quicker than I have. Before I got here, I never realized the enormity of the problem. I underestimated the number of reinforcements, like-minded fellow senators, that would be necessary for me to succeed.

I will keep doing my part. I will speak out every day against these despicable government bullies and their outrageous behavior. I will speak out against a government that harasses private property owners for no good reason. I will speak out against a government that throws small businessmen and -women in jail simply for trying to make a better life for their families and communities.

I will speak out against a government that fines and imprisons American citizens for breaking nebulous foreign laws and regulations. I will speak out against a government that harasses businesses for continuing with the same business practices they have for decades, that is, until some bureaucrat decides that they are breaking some arbitrary law.

I will speak against government agencies that basically

create their own laws to suit their own agendas. Our Constitution gives the role of making the laws of the nation to Congress—not unelected bureaucrats! I will speak out against government agencies that have gotten away with terrorizing American citizens for decades with no oversight or restraint from the courts or federal government.

I will speak out against a government that thinks groping, harassing, and humiliating airport travelers is simply the new norm in this country. The terrorists who attacked us on 9/11 hoped to frighten Americans into giving up their freedoms. I will speak out against government agencies like the TSA that have diminished our freedoms.

I will speak out against armed government SWAT teams that drag Amish dairy farmers from their beds at dawn simply for selling raw milk. I will speak out against arrogant bureaucrats who insist on punishing innocent citizens for the "crime" of selling rabbits. I will speak out against a government that favors corporate interests over family farms by hampering the latter with ridiculous and unnecessary regulations.

I will introduce the bills and amendments that could fix these problems and will fight for their passage. I will endorse candidates and work with elected officials who want to help me pass these bills and amendments. If they don't pass, I will introduce them again. And again. And support even more candidates and elected officials who want to help.

Whatever it takes.

I did not come to Washington, D.C., simply to make the trains run on time and protect the status quo. The status quo is broken. Worse, our federal government and its many tentacle agencies have become the enemy of the people as much if not more than they have been public servants. Americans don't want their hard-earned tax dollars going to a government that regularly works against their interests. To the degree that we must have government, it should be to help us, not hurt us.

Freedom can often be a vague term. But when we lose it, the definition immediately becomes concrete. I have shared with you many stories of everyday, hardworking Americans who've seen their freedom taken away from them in the blink of an eye, often without reason and without their having sufficient recourse. Our Constitution gives the federal government guidelines that are supposed to protect both our freedoms and also protect us from the government. I will fight to make our federal government follow the Constitution, as all elected officials take an oath to do, once again. The proper constitutional order must be restored, so that America is governed once again as the Founding Fathers intended.

I will keep fighting to protect the freedoms that belong to all American citizens as our birthright. I hope you'll join me.

Appendix: Notes and Sources

Many people and resources contributed to this book. While I have met or talked to many of these people personally, there are others whose stories were very powerful and needed to be amplified.

This book is not an investigative book. Many of the stories told and information reported represent work already done by others. Rather than endlessly noting multiple sourced items mixed in with personal conversations and research, we have included here other sources of information for the stories presented. Some are activist websites. Some are blogs. Some are reporters. Some are government websites with official releases of information. All of these sources contributed in one way or another to the finished material in this book, and I am grateful for the work many individuals have done in various fields to help expose these government bullies.

Live links to these and other sources of information are also located on www.governmentbullies.com, where you can also find pictures, video, and other information. This website is a good resource for those wanting to further delve into the seemingly endless reports on government bullying and news items related to the people and subjects covered in this book. There are even more stories to tell about the battles fought by John Pozsgai, Mike and Chantell Sackett, Robbie Wrigley, John Rapanos, Ocie Mills, Marinus Van Leuzen, Bill Ellen, Henry Juszkiewicz, David McNab, Abner Schoenwetter, Robert Blandford, Diane Huang, Steve and Cornelia Joyce Kinder, Nancy Okail, Sherif Mansour, Daniel Allgyer, John Moody, John and Judy Dollarhite, and others. There is additional information about the indignities suffered at the hands of the TSA by Owen JJ Stone, Carolyn Durand, Eliana Sutherland, Donna D'Errico, Susie Castillo, Thomas Sawyer, Tammy Banovac, Mandi Hamlin, Amy Strand, Ryan Thomas and Leona Thomas, and countless others like them.

Books

One of the foremost authors on regulatory and property rights is James DeLong. His books are indispensable to understanding the weight of these problems:

- *Property Matters: How Property Rights Are Under Assault and Why You Should Care*
- *Out of Bounds and Out of Control: Regulatory Enforcement at the EPA*

Another important author on regulations, food freedom, and other matters is farmer and lecturer Joel Salatin:

- *Folks, This Ain't Normal: A Farmer's Advice for Happier Hens, Healthier People, and a Better World*
- *Everything I Want to Do Is Illegal: War Stories from the Local Food Front*

Organizations and Websites

- Campaign for Liberty: www.campaignforliberty.com
- Pacific Legal Foundation: www.pacificlegal.org
- Heritage Foundation: www.Heritage.org
- American Land Rights Association: www.landrights.org
- Cato Institute: www.cato.org
- Overcriminalized: www.overcriminalized.com
- World Net Daily: www.worldnetdaily.com

While I may not agree with everything a group or website says, these groups and sites report on issues in this book in a way that the mainstream media often simply does not.

Primary Sources Categorized by Subject

James V. DeLong: Property Wrongs Articles

- Property Wrongs: A compilation of property abuse stories- http://jamesvdelong.com/books/stories.html

John Pozsgai

- "John Pozsgai" (obituary): "John Pozsgai died at his Morris-ville home surrounded by his wife, grandchildren and friends on Wednesday, Oct. 12, 2011. He was 79." http://www.phillyburbs. com/obituaries/courier_times/john-pozsgai/article_4ca54775 -0a3b-5e74-8864-eaf74847f5fc.html
- "Wetlands Enforcement": http://www.epa.gov/owow/wet lands/facts/fact15.html
- "What the EPA Did to John Pozsgai": http://voices.yahoo.com/ what-epa-did-john-pozsgai-10277431.html
- "Private Property Rights: An Endangered Species": http:// www.thefreemanonline.org/columns/private-property-rights -an-endangered-species/
- "Case Studies in Regulation: John Pozsgai": http://washington examiner.com/article/144015
- "Everyone Is a Potential Criminal in the Eyes of the EPA": http://reason.com/archives/2012/06/20/everybodys-a-poten tial-criminal-in-the-e
- "Sen. Rand Paul Holds Hearing on Government Assault on Pri-vate Property": http://www.louisville.com/content/sen-rand -paul-holds-hearing-government-assault-private-property-arena
- "If You Rearrange the Letters in EPA, It spells Schutzstaffel": http://www.freerepublic.com/focus/f-bloggers/2891811/posts
- "Excessive Regulations Are Killing the Economy and the Prospects for Jobs": http://www.conservativeactionalerts. com/2012/06/excessive-regulations-are-killing-the-economy -and-the-prospects-for-jobs/
- "Protecting Ecologically Valuable Wetlands Without Destroying Property Rights": http://www.heritage.org/research/reports/ 1991/07/bg840-protecting-ecologically-valuable-wetlands

John Rapanos

- "[T]he government was asking for more jail time for Mr. Rapanos than a drug dealer sentenced the same day. With clear outrage, Judge Zatkoff stated: 'So here we have a person who comes to the United States and commits crimes of selling dope and the gov-ernment asks me to put him in prison for 10 months. And then we have an American citizen who buys land, pays for it with his own money, and he moves some sand from one end to the other and the government wants me to give him 63 months in prison. Now, if that isn't our system gone crazy, I don't know what is. And I'm not going to do it.'" "PLF Tenacity Wins U.S. Supreme Court Review of Michigan Landowner's 'Wetlands' Case": http://heartland.org/sites/all/modules/custom/heartland _migration/files/pdfs/19322.pdf

- "Justice Scalia's Regrettably Irrelevant Decision in *Rapanos v. United States*": http://www.cato.org/pubs/articles/moller_rapanos-vs -u.s.pdf
- "The Clean Water Land Grab": http://www.cato.org/pubs/reg ulation/regv32n4/v32n4-5.pdf
- "Supreme Court 'Muddies' Wetlands Law": http://news.heart land.org/newspaper-article/2006/08/01/supreme-court-mud dies-wetlands-law
- "A False Dawn for Federalism: Clear Statement Rules After *Gonzales V. Raich*" (pp. 126–130 discuss *Rapanos*): http://papers .ssrn.com/sol3/papers.cfm?abstract_id=928985
- "*Rapanos* Case Muddies the Water": http://www.cato.org/mul timedia/daily-podcast/rapanos-case-muddies-water
- "Montana Senate to Feds: 'Leave Our Water Alone'": http:// news.heartland.org/newspaper-article/2009/04/01/montana- senate-feds-leave-our-water-alone
- "Town Battles Army Corps over Permafrost": http://news.heart land.org/newspaper-article/2006/12/01/town-battles-army -corps-over-permafrost

Mike and Chantell Sackett

- "The Sacketts bought a small parcel of about two-thirds of an acre in the Idaho Panhandle in 2005, near the shores of the resort community of Priest Lake. They hoped to build a three-bedroom home, surrounded by neighbors' houses, and had obtained a county permit. Gravel had already been laid for the foundation when EPA officials told them their land was a wetland. They were ordered to immediately 'restore' the land to its natural state or risk fines of up to $37,500 a day." "'Little Guy' Wins High Court Fight over Property Rights": http://articles.cnn.com/2012-03

-21/us/us_scotus-property-rights_1_property-rights-high-court
-clean-water-act?_s=PM:US

- "EPA's Enforcement Authority After *Sackett*: Same Old, Same Old": http://www.jdsupra.com/post/documentViewer.aspx?fid= 4eab5e3b-266f-4d1c-bef2-6a1a79841c94
- "PLF and the Sacketts take the EPA to Court": http://www .pacificlegal.org/Sackett
- "*Washington Post, SCOTUS Blog, L.A. Times* on Sackett Case": http://blog.pacificlegal.org/2012/washington-post-scotus -blog-on-sackett-cas/
- "*Sackett v. EPA*: The Real Story": http://blog.pacificlegal .org/2012/sackett-v-epa-the-real-rest-of-the-story/
- PDF of Chantell's physical letters to the EPA: http://blog.paci ficlegal.org/wordpress/wp-content/uploads/2012/04/Sack ettnotes.pdf
- PDF of the Sacketts' declaration before the Supreme Court: http:// blog.pacificlegal.org/wordpress/wp-content/uploads/2012/ 04/Sackettdeclaration.pdf
- "Compliance—or Else": http://www.cato.org/pubs/regula tion/regv34n4/v34n4-2.pdf
- "EPA Actions Should Be Subject to Judicial Review": http:// www.cato-at-liberty.org/epa-actions-should-be-subject-to-judi cial-review/
- "*Sackett v. EPA*: Supreme Court Takes Up Property Rights Case": http://blog.heritage.org/2012/01/09/sackett-v-epa-supreme -court-takes-up-property-rights-case/
- "*Washington Post*: EPA Earns Reputation for Abuse": http:// blog.heritage.org/2012/05/04/washington-post-epa-earning -a-reputation-for-abuse/
- "How One Couple Took On the EPA and Ended Up in the Supreme Court": http://blog.heritage.org/2012/01/07/scribe cast-how-one-couple-took-on-epa-and-ended-up-at-supreme -court/
- "Priest Lake, Idaho Property Rights Amicus": http://www .ij.org/sackett-v-epa

Robbie Wrigley

- "Now the nightmare is over. But it is still a bad dream. Her 70-year-old father and his 80-year-old engineer are still imprisoned.

Her main concern now is freeing them." "A Nightmare Is Over": http://www.enterprise-journal.com/opinion/article_2db7a8e6 -ccc9-11df-a462-001cc4c03286.html

- "Woman Convicted of EPA Crimes Released from Prison": http://www.winonatimes.com/view/full_story/9813731/arti cle-Woman-convicted-of-EPA-crimes-released-from-prison
- EPAcasefiles:http://www.epa.gov/compliance/resources/cases/ criminal/highlights/2006/bighillacres.pdf
- "3 Individuals and 2 Corporations Found Guilty": http://www. greenenvironmentnews.com/Environment/Agriculture/3+Indi viduals+and+2+Corporations+Found+Guilty+in+Mississippi+W etlands+Case
- "41 Count Indictment in Mississippi Wetlands Case": http:// www.greenenvironmentnews.com/Environment/Agriculture/4 1+Count+Indictment+in+Mississippi+Wetlands+Contamination +Case
- "Fifth Circuit Upholds Wetlands Conviction": http://masglp .olemiss.edu/Water%20Log/WL28/28.1wetlands.htm

Ocie Mills

- "After beginning construction on the foundation of his water-front home, federal agents cited Ocie for polluting navigable waters of the United States. Ocie had previously secured a county permit for his house and state inspectors had marked the area of shoreline that was protected. This evidence was disallowed on the basis of the supremacy of the federal agency over the local and state governments. Ocie and his son each served 21 month prison sentences. Later a federal judge determined the property was 'probably never a wetland for purposes of the Clean Water Act.'" "Ocie's 'Land of the Free...'": http://www.wnd .com/1999/09/5415/
- *Ocie Mills and Carey Mills v. United States of America*: http:// www.justice.gov/osg/briefs/2000/0responses/2000-0722 .resp.html
- "Ocie Mills' Government Fight Covers 20 Years: Heads Back to Court": http://www.propertyrightsresearch.org/ocie_mills .htm
- "Fined, Convicted and Locked Up for 21 Months": http://www .couldyoubenext.com/ociemills.htm

Marinus Van Leuzen

- "After Marinus Van Leuzen, a 73-year-old immigrant from Holland, attempted to build his retirement home on a bit of property he had owned for more than 20 years, Van Leuzen was charged with depositing illegal fill material on the property. The Army Corps of Engineers cited Section 404 of the Clean Water Act which requires a person to obtain a permit before filling a "navigable water" of the United States. Mr. Van Leuzen was forced to pay significant fines and restore the property and faced further charges after Corps deemed Mr. Van Leuzen had not planted the proper vegetation while restoring his property." "A Sign of the Times": http://cei.org/op-eds-articles/sign-times
- "The photos below illustrate the documentation of the bizarre, cruel order by Judge Samuel B. Kent, US District court, Galveston, where he compared Marinus Van Leuzen's supposed infringement on a 0.4 acre wetland to the 'genocidal treatment of this continent's indigenous peoples.'" "Marinus Van Leuzen Courageous in Youth and Old Age": http://prfamerica.org/van leuzen/VanLeuzenPhotos.html
- "Wetlands Reform and the Criminal Enforcement Record: A Cautionary Tale": http://lawreview.wustl.edu/inprint/76-1/761-06.html

Bill Ellen

- "Ellen served 6 months in jail for failing to comply with regulations regarding wetland use. Bill Ellen was attempting to alter the wetland to make it a more attractive environment for geese and ducks in hopes of establishing a hunting reserve, and in doing so caused no irreparable damage to the wetland. Instead of being forced to repair the wetlands to original condition, he was sentenced to spend the holidays in prison." "Clinton's Next Task: Free Bill Ellen": http://articles.baltimoresun.com/1993-01-25/news/1993025170_1_muskrats-wetlands-ellen
- "Swamp Rules: The End of Federal Wetland Regulation?": https://www.cato.org/pubs/regulation/regv22n2/swamprules.pdf
- "Protection Against Federal Regulatory Abuse": http://www.cato.org/publications/congressional-testimony/protection-against-federal-regulatory-abuse

John and Judy Dollarhite

- "But now, selling a few hundred rabbits over two years has provoked the heavy hand of the federal government to the tune of a $90,643 fine. The fine was levied more than a year after authorities contacted family members, prompting them to immediately halt their part-time business and liquidate their equipment." "USDA Fines Family $90k for Selling Rabbits Without a License": http://dailycaller.com/2011/05/24/usda-fines-missouri-family-90k-for-selling-a-few-rabbits-without-a-license/
- "Dollarhite Story Tells Us All We Need to Know bout Our Government": http://www.leftcoastrebel.com/2011/05/missouri-dollarhite-bunny-farm-tells-us.html
- "Dollarhites' Testimony: Property Wrongs—10/12/11": http://www.youtube.com/watch?v=OzJ1cn0-oT0
- "Update on the Dollarhites": http://www.iheardthepeoplesay.org/2011/11/25/update-on-the-dollarhites/
- "USDA Stands Behind Hare-Raising Fine": http://bobmccarty.com/2011/05/19/usda-stands-behind-hare-raising-fine/

Daniel Allgyer:

- "FDA Wins two year fight to shut down Amish farmer for selling raw milk across state lines. Mr. Allgyer was subject to an unannounced 5 A.M. inspection by the FDA, a "straw purchase sting operation," and faces significant fines if he continues to violate the law." "Feds Shut Down Amish Farm for Selling Fresh Milk": http://www.washingtontimes.com/news/2012/feb/13/feds-shut-down-amish-farm-selling-fresh-mi/
- "Farmer Ordered to Stop Interstate Sales of Raw Milk": http://www.philly.com/philly/news/breaking/139373933.html
- "Amish Milk: The Latest Target of the Obama Regulatory State": http://blog.heritage.org/2011/04/30/amish-milk-the-latest-target-of-the-obama-regulatory-state/
- "Raw Milk Rebellion": http://www.cato.org/publications/commentary/raw-milk-rebellion
- "I Got Hooked on the White Stuff Back in the '70s": http://www.cato-at-liberty.org/i-got-hooked-on-the-white-stuff-back-in-the-70s/

- "Should This Milk be Legal?": http://www.nytimes.com/2007/08/08/dining/08raw.html?_r=1&pagewanted=2&ei=5087%0A&em&en=0d797ce6edce7564&ex=1186804800
- "President Obama's War on Fun": http://www.cato.org/publications/commentary/president-obamas-war-fun

Honduran Fishermen

- "In 1999, agents of the National Marine Fisheries Service, acting on a tip, seized one of McNab's shipments in Alabama. They found that about 4 percent of the lobsters were undersized, 7 percent were egg-bearing, and all were packaged in plastic bags rather than boxes. In consultation with the Honduran Ministry of Agriculture and Livestock, the federal agents determined that the shipment was in violation of Honduran (not American) law." "Pardon Libby? Maybe, but Not Alone: Why David Henson McNab Deserves Clemency": http://reason.com/archives/2007/04/02/pardon-libby-maybe-but-not-alo
- "Case Studies: *McNab v. United States*": http://www.overcriminalized.com/casestudy/McNab-Imprison-by-Foreign-Laws.aspx
- "McNab to Continue Serving Federal Prison Sentence for Lobster Smuggling": http://www.publicaffairs.noaa.gov/releases2004/mar04/noaa04-r119.html
- *United States of America, Plaintiff-Appellee, versus David Henson McNab*, United States District Court for the Southern District of Alabama: http://uniset.ca/other/cs3/331F3d1228.html
- *McNab v. United States of America* and *Blandford, Schoenwetter, and Huang v. United States of America*:
- http://www.forestlegality.org/files/fla/lacey_case_mcnab_vs_us.pdf
- "Begging His Pardon": http://www.cato.org/publications/commentary/begging-pardon
- "Four Involved in Lobster Harvesting and Distribution Found Guilty in Illegal Import Scheme": http://www.justice.gov/opa/pr/2000/November/647enrd.htm

Foreign Bullies

- "It's fairly appropriate, then, that one of the defendants, Freedom House Egypt director, Nancy Okail, was captured by the

European Press photo Agency reading George Orwell through the black bars of the cage where the accused stand during trial. Orwell is famous for his anti-authoritarian works, *Animal Farm* and *1984*, as commentaries on thought control and government surveillance and propaganda." "Egypt: Reading Orwell in the Dock": http://www.globalpost.com/dispatches/globalpost-blogs/the-middle-east/egypt-ngo-trial-orwell-freedom-house

- "Defendants accused of working for unlicensed non-governmental organizations (NGOs) and receiving illegal foreign funds, stand in a cage during the opening of their trial, in Cairo, Egypt, 26 February 2012. Most defendants stay away as NGO trial opens in Cairo on 26 February, just six of the 43 defendants turned up in court for the first session of the trial. In December 2011, Egyptian police raided the offices of 17 NGOs across the country, detaining employees and seizing computer files." "Egypt Opens Trial That Has Strained Ties with US": http://www.vosizneias.com/news/photos/view/830245833

- "Egypt Says It Will Lift Travel Ban, Allowing American Defendants to Leave": http://www.nytimes.com/2012/03/01/world/middleeast/egypt-says-it-will-lift-travel-ban-allowing-accused-americans-to-leave.html?pagewanted=all

- "Nancy Okail Discusses Egypt's NGO Crackdown": http://www.freedomhouse.org/blog/nancy-okail-discusses-egypts-ngo-crackdown

- "Why Egypt Moved Against Unregistered NGOs": http://www.washingtonpost.com/opinions/why-egypt-moved-against-unregistered-ngos/2012/03/05/gIQAEHrf1R_story.html

- "Egypt's War on NGOs": http://www.thedailybeast.com/newsweek/2012/02/05/egypt-cracks-down-on-ngos.html

- "Egypt's NGO Crisis: How Will US Aid Play in the Controversy?": http://www.time.com/time/world/article/0,8599,2106420,00.html#ixzz1znetLpAR

- "Egypt NGO Law Could Undermine Freedoms: U.N. Rights Chief": http://w03O18J20120425

Gibson Guitar

- "'Can you imagine a federal agent saying, "You're going to jail for five years" and what you do is sort wood in the factory?' said

Mr. Juszkiewicz, recounting the incident. 'I think that's way over the top.' Gibson employees, he said, are being 'treated like drug criminals.'" "Gibson Guitar Wails on Federal Raid over Wood": http://online.wsj.com/article/SB10001424053111903895904 576542942027859286.html

- "Gibson Case Drags On with No Sign of Criminal Charges": http://www.foxnews.com/us/2012/04/12/gibson-guitar-case -drags-on-with-no-sign-criminal-charges/
- "Why Gibson Guitar Was Raided by the Justice Department": http://www.npr.org/blogs/therecord/2011/08/31/ 140090116/why-gibson-guitar-was-raided-by-the-justice -department
- The Great Gibson Guitar Raid: Months Later, Still No Charges Filed": http://reason.com/blog/2012/02/23/the-great-gibson -guitar-raid-months-late
- "House to Vote on Easing Environmental Regulations After Gibson Guitar Raid": http://thehill.com/blogs/e2-wire/e2 -wire/229545-house-to-vote-on-easing-environmental-regula tions-after-gibson-guitar-raid
- "Whose Axe Made Your Axe? You Better Find Out": http:// www.cato-at-liberty.org/whose-axe-made-your-axe-you-better -find-out/
- "Reason.tv on Gibson's Ongoing Battle with the Federal Government": http://www.cato-at-liberty.org/reason-tv-on-gibsons -ongoing-battle-with-the-federal-government/
- "Gibson Guitar CEO Slams US Raid as 'Overreach'": http:// www.reuters.com/article/2011/10/12/us-guitar-idUSTRE79 B7PT20111012

John Moody

- "Just after New Year's Day, the Obama administration gave its official response of 'No!' to the 6,078 signers of a petition on WhiteHouse. gov who requested federal-level legalization of all raw milk sales." "Obama Administration Says 'No Raw Milk for You'": http://www .farmtoconsumer.org/obama-admin-says-no-raw-milk.htm
- "FDA Throws Raw Milk Freedom Riders a Bone, but What We Really Want...": http://www.foodclubsandcoops.com/fda-throws -raw-milk-freedom-riders-a-bone-but-what-we-really-want/51/

- "Food Freedom Legal Battles Rage": http://rockrivertimes
.com/2012/02/22/food-freedom-legal-battles-rage/

Steve and Cornelia Joyce Kinder

- "Steve T. Kinder, 51, and Kinder Caviar Inc. with illegally harvesting paddlefish from Ohio waters and falsely reporting to
the Kentucky Department of Fish & Wildlife Resources that he
caught the fish in Kentucky; and Cornelia Joyce Kinder, 53, as
well as Kinder Caviar Inc. and Black Star Caviar Company with
providing false information about the paddlefish eggs to the U.S.
Fish & Wildlife Service in order to obtain permits to export the
paddlefish eggs to foreign customers, including the amount of
paddlefish eggs to be exported, the names of the fishermen that
harvested the paddlefish and the location where the paddlefish
were harvested." "The Great Kentucky Caviar Criminal Caper
Comes to an End in Ohio": http://www.forbes.com/sites/bills
inger/2012/01/18/the-great-kentucky-caviar-criminal-caper
-comes-to-an-end-in-ohio/
- "Husband-Wife Team Admit Illegally Selling Paddlefish Caviar":
http://www.ens-newswire.com/ens/jan2012/2012-01-17-093
.html
- "Kentuckians Convicted of Lacey Act Crimes for Illegally Harvesting and Making False Records for Ohio River Paddlefish":
http://www.justice.gov/opa/pr/2012/January/12-enrd-059
.html
- Kentucky Couple Charged with Lacey Act Crimes Based on the
Illegal Harvest of Paddlefish from the Ohio River": http://www
.justice.gov/opa/pr/2011/March/11-enrd-325.html

TSA

- "A Texas woman who said she was forced to remove a nipple ring
with pliers in order to board an airplane called Thursday for an
apology by federal security agents and a civil rights investigation.
'I wouldn't wish this experience upon anyone,' Mandi Hamlin
said at a news conference. 'My experience with TSA was a nightmare I had to endure. No one deserves to be treated this way.'"

"TSA Forces Woman to Remove Nipple Rings": http://www
.cbsnews.com/stories/2008/03/27/travel/main3976376.shtml
- "The TSA's invasive new screening measures include officers literally putting their hands down people's pants if they are wearing baggy clothing in a shocking new elevation of groping procedures that have stoked a nationwide revolt against privacy-busting airport security measures." "TSA Now Putting Hands Down Fliers' Pants": http://www.prisonplanet.com/tsa-now-putting-hands-down-fliers-pants.html
- "Bully TSA Agents at LAX": http://www.tsascanthis.com/2010/11/17/bully-tsa-agents-at-lax/
- "Daniel Rubin: An Infuriating Search at Philadelphia International Airport": http://www.tsascanthis.com/2010/11/29/daniel-rubin-an-infuriating-search-at-philadelphia-international-airport/
- "TSA Grabs Junk": http://www.outsidethebeltway.com/tsa-grabs-junk/
- "Former Miss USA: I Was Molested by TSA Agent in Dallas": http://www.outsidethebeltway.com/former-miss-usa-i-was-molested-by-a-tsa-agent-in-dallas/
- "TSA Agent Spills Grandfather's Ashes in Confrontation with Passenger": http://www.rawstory.com/rs/2012/06/26/tsa-agent-spills-grandfathers-ashes-in-confrontation-with-passenger/
- "'They Were Staring Me Up and Down': Woman Claimed US Airport Security Staff Singled Her Out for Her Breasts": http://www.dailymail.co.uk/news/article-1333090/Woman-claimed-TSA-security-staff-singled-breasts.html#ixzz1zqubrr88
- "More TSA Misery as Wheelchair-Bound Woman in Lingerie Gets Hour-Long Search and Misses Flight": http://www.dailymail.co.uk/news/article-1334937/Tammy-Banovac-wheelchair-bound-woman-wearing-lingerie-gets-hour-long-airport-search.html#ixzz1zqunilTL
- "Why Pick Me for a 'Nude' Security Scan?: Ex-*Baywatch* Star Claims Airport Staff Were Leering at Her Contours": http://www.dailymail.co.uk/news/article-1336331/Baywatchs-Donna-DErrico-picked-nude-TSA-body-scan-airport-staff-leered.html#ixzz1zqvlYPC0
- "TSA Under Fire After Businessman Boards International Flight with Loaded Handgun": http://www.dailymail.co.uk/news/

article-1339513/U-S-security-comes-businessman-boards
-international-flight-loaded-handgun.html#ixzz1zqvFKTdM

- "My Sex Life with the TSA": http://www.huffingtonpost.com/
naomi-wolf/my-sex-life-with-the-tsa_b_868020.html
- "Breaking News: Rand Paul Detained by the TSA": http://www
.examiner.com/article/breaking-news-rand-paul-detained-by-tsa
- "4-Year-Old Gets TSA Patdown After a Hug from her Grandmother": http://www.examiner.com/article/4-year-old-gets-tsa
-patdown-after-a-hug-from-her-grandmother
- "Senator Rand Paul Detained After Refusing TSA Pat-down at
Nashville Airport": http://www.examiner.com/article/senator
-rand-paul-detained-after-refusing-tsa-pat-down-at-nashville
-airport
- "TSA Patting Down a 3-Year-Old in a Wheelchair": http://
www.examiner.com/article/video-of-tsa-patting-down-3-year
-old-wheelchair
- "Newark Airport Security Screener Charged with Stealing $495
from Passenger's Purse": http://www.nj.com/news/index.ssf/
2010/05/security_scanner_at_newark_air.html
- "Baker County Woman Sues After Rolex Goes Missing at
Norfolk Airport": http://jacksonville.com/news/metro/2010
-05-23/story/woman-sues-over-missing-24000-watch-after-air
port-security-check#ixzz1zqzLuhrf
- "TSA Supervisor Allegedly Stole Cash from Passenger Bags":
http://abcnews.go.com/Travel/michael-arato-tsa-supervisor
-allegedly-stole-cash-passenger/story?id=11927122
- "Another Terrorist Stopped by Vigilant TSA Officer: 4-Year-Old
Boy in Leg Braces": http://www.cbsnews.com/8301-504083
_162-6212730-504083.html
- "TSA Pats Down 3-Year-Old": http://www.newser.com/story/
105351/tsa-pats-down-3-year-old.html
- "TSA Stands by Officers After Pat-down of Elderly Woman in Florida": http://www.cnn.com/2011/US/06/26/florida.tsa.incide
nt/index.html?iref=allsearch
- "TSA Has No Decency": http://www.campaignforliberty.org/
profile/7786/blog/2012/06/26/tsa-has-no-decency
- "Recapping Rand's TSA Encounter": http://www.campaignfor
liberty.org/profile/7786/blog/2012/01/24/recapping-rands
-tsa-encounter

- "The TSA Is Bad for Your Health": http://www.campaignforlib erty.org/node/11534
- "Are You Feeling Safer?": http://www.campaignforliberty.org/ profile/7780/blog/2011/08/22/are-you-feeling-safer
- "This Could Be Your Grandmother!": http://www.campaign forliberty.org/profile/7786/blog/2011/07/15/could-be-your -grandmother
- "Just How 'Secure' Is Airport Security?": http://www.cam paignforliberty.org/profile/7788/blog/2012/03/13/test

Acknowledgments

I could not even begin to acknowledge the debt I and all Americans owe to the men and women in this book. Many of them I have met personally. All of their stories have moved me and spurred me to greater action.

We all face intrusive government in our daily lives, from something as simple as the DMV, to the IRS, or the local zoning board. Those who stand up and fight against something as large and powerful as their own government deserve our thanks, and they deserve to have their stories be a catalyst for change.

I would like to thank my family for their ever-present love and support, and for tolerating the schedule and life of the U.S. Senate. Every week I leave my wife, Kelley, and our boys, William, Duncan, and Robert, to fight against a state that has created the stories in this book. I hope that, as they read them, they remember why this battle is so imporant. I know I remember why it is so important every time I look at them.

A thank you also to the family of my chief of staff and co-author, Doug Stafford, his wife, Elizabeth, and his four children, for putting up with even longer hours and work more than usual while working on this book.

To the best staff on Capitol Hill: I am humbled every day by your dedication to our cause and hard work toward our goals.

There is no doubt I could not do this without all of you. Particular thanks go to Rachel Bovard, who spends much of her time fighting the EPA with me; and to Eleanor May, for her able research assistance and help putting together this book.

To Rolf Zettersten, Kate Hartson, and everyone at Hachette, especially Bob Castillo and his production team. It is always a pleasure to work with you. Thank you for your encouragement on the topic of this book, your guidance through the process of putting it together, and your patience in allowing us the time we needed to get it right with our busy schedule in the Senate. Thanks also to Jack Hunter for joining the team and adding his editorial help.

A special note of praise and thanks to the groups who fight alongside the men and women in this book. Many of them are lawyers who defended these heroes or activists who helped make sure fewer people have to fight in the future.

Among the groups I have gotten to know are Campaign for Liberty on issues like the TSA, Pacific Research Institute, Institute for Justice, the American land rights association in defense of property and individual rights, Freedom House and International Republican Institute, whose men and women were detained in Egypt for promoting freedom. All of you and many others not named here are on the front lines of this battle. I hope that by telling more of these stories, we can help make your job easier, and bring liberty to more people here and abroad.

To those who inspired me through their earlier works: Specific details are cited in the endnotes, but generally I wish to thank James DeLong, author of *Property Matters* and *Out of Bounds, Out of Control.* Thanks also to Gene Healey of Cato and Brian Walsh of Heritage for their work in the area of overregulation, especially the excellent resource www.overcriminalized

.com Also to the following websites that report stories the mainstream media often passes by: naturalnews.com, mercola.com, worldnetdaily.com, campaignforliberty.org, and many others.

I urge those who read this book to keep up with those sites as well as our new www.governmentbullies.com site, to learn more about these and other stories.